Dermot Gardens

Dermot O'Neill

POOLBEG

Published 2003
Poolbeg Press Ltd.
123 Grange Hill, Baldoyle,
Dublin 13, Ireland
Email: poolbeg@poolbeg.com

© Dermot O'Neill 2003

The moral right of the author has been asserted.

Copyright for typesetting, layout, design
© Poolbeg Group Services Ltd.

A catalogue record for this book is available from the British Library.

ISBN 1-84223-065-4

Photographs by Dermot O'Neill
Designed by Steven Hope
Typeset by Patricia Hope

Printed by Nørhaven Book,
Viborg, Denmark

www.poolbeg.com

Biography

Dermot O'Neill is one of Ireland's best-loved gardening personalities. His passion and enthusiasm for his subject touches many people and his down-to-earth, colourful, easy to follow style brings the joy of gardening to a wide audience. His keen interest in all growing things started early in childhood when Dermot's grandmother guided and encouraged him to grow plants from seed and also tend a gardening patch. These early results developed into a passion then to an all-absorbing career.

Closely associated with Open House Dermot is also the voice of gardening on *Today with Pat Kenny* on Radio One.

Dermot has been very keenly involved with gardening and horticultural societies both at home and abroad. He is a member of twenty-eight international organisations and at home he has been a founder committee member of the Irish Garden Plants Society. He is also a past council member of the Royal Horticultural Society of Ireland and recently he has been made a Special Friend of the Garden and Landscape Designers Association.

Dermot can be found online at **www.dermotoneill.com**, where he is delighted to receive your input and gardening queries.

Acknowledgements

I would like to thank Bill O'Sullivan for his support and advice in the preparation of this book. I would like to acknowledge the encouragement of all of my gardening friends, especially the support of Carmel Duignan, Brian O'Donnell, John Cushnie and Thomas Quarney.

A special mention to Stephen Smith for his generous support.

Also, a special thank you to Helen and Val Dillon for their ongoing support and for allowing me to photograph many of the plants at their garden, 45 Sandford Road, Ranelagh.

To Patricia Carroll and Michael Scott of Tyrone Productions, who have made this book possible. To Marty Whelan and Mary Kennedy, whose weekly encouragement is always supportive. To the series producer Larry Masterson, Bernie O'Connor, Mark O'Neill, Anna Dillon and all the producers and directors, researchers and the team who make up the Open House office.

A word of thanks must go to all the garden centres and nurserymen who so kindly help me with my weekly displays on Open House.

I would like to dedicate this book to my parents who have always encouraged my interest in gardening and whose support I know I can always rely on.

Introduction

I find it hard to believe that I started gardening on afternoon television twenty-one years ago. Back then, it was believed to be impossible to do a regular weekly gardening item on television throughout the winter months. Luckily, I was given the opportunity to prove this theory wrong and I set about on a weekly basis bringing gardening information, tips and advice into people's homes.

This all started with the programme *Live at Three* and today I am still gardening on afternoon television every Thursday on *Open House* with Marty and Mary.

What few people realise is the tremendous amount of work that goes into preparing the gardening items on *Open House*. I usually plan ahead 3-4 weeks so that I can keep the gardening items topical and relevant to what's happening in your own garden. I visit nurseries, garden centres, and growers searching for the latest plants and the newest ideas, which I can bring to viewers. There is an enormous team of people behind the scenes who help bring the programme to you – directors, producers, researchers, cameramen, sound technicians, lighting, designers, floor managers, stagehands, are just some of the many different experts who are needed to bring you live television.

Mounting a weekly display involves quite a lot of co-ordination, selecting plants and items to be brought to studio, co-ordinating transport, and early on a Thursday morning the job starts of setting up the display once everything has been delivered. I set about with a group of people preparing the display, organising the sequence, rehearsing with cameras, and of course discussing with Marty and Mary the gardening topic of the day. By the time we go live on air several days work has already gone into the preparation of the item you are about to see. RTÉ has pioneered a live studio-based weekly gardening item. No other live television programme provides such a detailed and well-planned weekly gardening item for its viewers and this has stood to the popularity of Thursday's gardening item on *Open House*.

I believe that gardening is accessible to everyone. Even those without a garden can still manage to grow an indoor plant and have the pleasure of something growing in their own home. No matter what your level of interest, whether you are a beginner or an expert, you can access the hobby of gardening at whatever level you wish and gain great pleasure and enjoyment from the activity of growing and appreciating plants. On *Open House*, I believe it is important to bring viewers gardening information which is simple and easy to follow. It is essential to demystify ordinary, simple gardening tasks. Over the series it is important that viewers discover the best seasonal plants they can grow in their gardens. It is also important that they learn simple gardening techniques – the best way to water, how to prune a rose, and even how to grow plants from seed. These are all essential and popular items on the show.

This book will act as a companion for *Open House* viewers and will give added information and act as a reference for many of the topics covered throughout the series. At the same time the information in the book is also valuable to any Irish gardener, whether they follow the programme or not. It may be just simply to refer to roses I have recommended or to discover what care is needed for a new lawn. The book has been designed in an easy-to-follow format. It will guide you and inspire you to get the most from your own gardens.

This book is a celebration of my twenty-one years gardening live on afternoon television. Here I share my gardening wisdom with all those who have followed my gardening television journey. This is a book for Irish gardeners experiencing Irish gardening conditions, be it our weather or our soil. It is a book to be enjoyed, dipped in and out of, and most of all a book which helps you get the most pleasure from your garden.

Relax and enjoy your garden

Contents

Acid soil in raised beds

Soil

The secret of successful gardening is caring for your soil. If you look after your soil everything else in your garden will do well. I have found that so many new gardeners neglect this area, as they are more interested and excited about plants.

Japanese azaleas and rhododendrons at Shirley Beatty's garden, Knockcree, enjoying lime-free soil

They often fail to deal with one of the fundamentals of good gardening and that is preparing the ground in advance of planting and generally looking after their garden soil. The gardeners of yesteryear understood this well and believed that if you spent a shilling on a plant it was important to spend a pound on the soil. To understand this will make a huge difference to the quality of your gardening. It will guarantee that your plants grow well and that your garden will continue to thrive. I cannot over-

Deciduous azalea *Rhododendron luteum*

stress the importance of enriching your garden soil. This is where every gardener should start.

Testing Your Soil's pH

Your garden soil will either be alkaline, acid or neutral, so it is important before you start planting to ascertain which category it falls into. This can be done with a simple pH test of your soil. The result will dictate what plants are most suited to growing in your garden.

A neutral soil is a pH of 7. Numbers lower than 7 indicate that your soil is acidic, suitable then for growing rhododendrons, azaleas, camellias, and a huge range of lime-hating plants. A number higher than 7 will indicate that your soil is alkaline. The common term for this is 'limey'.

Most garden centres sell pH kits. These are inexpensive to buy and extremely simple to use.

The majority of soils will fall between a pH of 6 and 8. It can be very difficult to change the pH of your soil. The addition of sulphur chips can help to change an alkaline soil to acid, but this can take time and may not always be totally satisfactory. You can add lime to increase the pH, but be careful not to overdo this.

Camellia 'Saint Ewe'– ideal for growing in lime-free compost in a container

Mulching

A mulch is a layer of organic matter spread on the soil surface around your plants. It helps to keep your soil moist in summer. Some mulches provide plant foods. It can help to reduce the attack of black spot on roses. It seals in weed seed and cuts down on weeding. And it greatly improves the quality and texture of your soil.

Bark

Bark comes in different grades, from fine to coarse. The fine composted bark decomposes quickly. The larger, coarser barks take longer to break down and remain visible and functional over many months.

Bark looks attractive and when initially applied often gives a pleasant woodland scent. You will need to choose between fine and coarse, remembering that fine will need to be added a little more thickly.

Manure

Traditionally, manure has been added to gardens. It is invaluable for the nutrients it adds to soil. Straw-based manure is far superior to manure which contains sawdust. Manure with sawdust can remove nitrogen from your soil as it decomposes. Fresh manure should never be used. It is important that manure is allowed to decompose well for a minimum of three months, if not left up to one year before being applied.

Compost

Making your own compost from garden and kitchen waste is now very fashionable but also an incredibly useful form of recycling waste matter. I encourage everybody to make their own garden compost. It makes a superb mulch and by keen gardeners is regarded as valuable as a bucket of gold. If you make it yourself, it is free. It is very high in valuable nutrients. Its only drawback is that it needs to be applied thickly to prevent weeds growing.

Cocoa Shells

This is a by-product from the manufacture of chocolate and is a renewable resource. It looks wonderful and smells wonderful too. It is necessary when you apply this to damp it with water to prevent it blowing away. Once wet, it binds together forming a dense porous mat. It is good at suppressing weeds and can be freshened up occasionally with a light sprinkling of fresh cocoa shell, which is an attractive brown colour.

Gravel

Gravel is widely available and comes in a wide choice of different types. It will not contribute any nutrients to your soil, but is an excellent way to retain moisture and provide essential drainage for plants which need these conditions. It is always a good idea to dig in plenty of manure or garden compost in advance of applying gravel. It is also a

Rhododendron 'Blue Diamond' surrounded by bark mulch to suppress weeds

good idea to apply a membrane of landscape fabric so that the gravel does not mix with your soil. It is also easier to add plants to a gravelled area by pulling the gravel to one side and cutting this fabric. The gravel then can be replaced and the plant will grow away happily.

Compost

The very best thing that you can do for your soil is to add lots of organic matter. Apart from adding well-rotted manure and other organic matters which are available through garden centres, it is a good idea to add your own garden compost. The results of this compost are fantastic and I believe it is worth many times its own weight in gold. It is a good idea to make a compost heap or have a

Rhododendron 'Polar Bear'– one of the very best
late-flowering large rhododendrons

compost bin in an out of the way corner of your garden. Into this you add a mixture of chopped up garden and kitchen waste and after several months this will decompose into a beautiful rich compost which can be used when planting, for mulching and generally to improve the quality of your soil.

Avoid building up a mass of green material such as grass cuttings as, in summer, these will rot down rapidly, making a smelly mess. The key to making quality, odourless, crumbly compost is the mixing of two different components: "brown material", for example twigs, chopped up woody pieces, prunings, dead plant material, with "green material" like annual weeds, grass, and kitchen waste.

It is possible to speed up and improve the process of decomposition by adding a compost activator. These usually contain nitrogen, which encourages the bacteria to rot everything down. It is also a good idea to chop up and to mix your materials well.

Compost is usually ready to use after about six months. In summer, when temperatures are warm, the process speeds up. But in winter, when the temperature is cooler, the process slows down. It is important in winter months to cover the top of the heap to prevent rain cooling the rotting process.

Potting Compost

Potting compost is completely different and totally unlike garden compost, which you use to improve your soil. Potting compost is sold in garden centres and is used for potting plants. The majority of these are made with peat with added nutrients. They have no extra feed value and it is most important when buying to make sure that the bag is fresh.

Multi-purpose Compost

This is an ideal potting compost which is suitable for growing plants in on a short term basis of up to one year. After this, it is best added to your compost heap. It is necessary to liquid-feed plants once they have established in their pots as, at this stage, the nutrients added to the peat may be running low.

Loam-based Compost

This type of compost is usually sold as 'John Innes' compost. In this case, it is based on soil with some

Rhododendron 'Nancy Evans'– happily growing
in a large pot of ericaceous compost

camellias, but it is not ideal for growing them on a long-term basis. If at all possible, look for a lime-free compost which contains loam as this will help to sustain the lime-hating shrub in the container for a greater length of time. It will also be necessary to liquid feed with an appropriate feed suitable for lime-hating plants. Little and often being advisable.

Compost heap at the Dillon Garden, 45 Sandford Road

peat and fertiliser added. It will hold onto its nutritional value much longer. It is also a heavier compost and I recommend it for longer-term plants such as trees and shrubs which grow in containers.

Growbags
These are ideal for growing tomatoes and salad crops. There are only enough nutrients in the grow bag to get the plants started. Therefore, it is important to use a liquid feed on a regular basis once plants have established.

Ericaceous Compost
This peat compost is made without the addition of lime, making it ideal for lime-haters such as

Wicker compost bin

Hints

Improving clay soil

Improve a clay soil by double digging, little by little, and incorporating masses of organic matter – it is the only reliable way.

What's your pH?

You will get an indication of the pH of your garden soil by looking at the wild plants growing nearby – for instance, rhododendrons indicate high acidity and clematis (old man's beard) high alkalinity.

Don't lime when you manure

Never apply lime and manure to the soil at the same time because they will react together to produce harmful ammonia. Allow at least two months to elapse between the two operations.

Increasing acidity

The only reliable way to increase the acidity of a naturally alkaline soil is by adding sulphur; peat will not make any difference unless added in unrealistically large quantities. Check with the manufacturer's directions for the amounts of sulphur required on different types of soil.

Iron deficiency

Dark green leaf veins combined with abnormally yellowed foliage is a symptom of iron deficiency, especially significant on limey soils and corrected by application of sequestered iron.

Autumn digging

When digging the soil in autumn, don't make the mistake of breaking down the clods too much for the winter rains will then only form a compacted surface. Leave the clods rough for nature to disintegrate slowly.

The right way with a spade

Always push a spade into the ground with the ball of your foot, not with the instep; and whenever possible use leather boots, not wellingtons, for digging.

Old-fashioned wooden wheelbarrow in the walled garden at Glenveagh Castle, Co. Donegal

Potting shed

Tools & Equipment

When starting out gardening for the first time it is important to have the right tools and equipment for the job. Having the right equipment guarantees you ease of work, so it is vital that you have the essentials before starting. Today garden centres offer a vast range, but you only need buy a few items to begin with. The basic tool kit includes a spade and fork to dig, a trowel and hand fork for smaller work between plants, a rake for preparing ground, a hoe for weeding, a shears for trimming hedges and grass, and a pair of secateurs for pruning. You will also find a wheelbarrow useful and it is a good idea to have a large piece of canvas or strong plastic sheeting for moving clippings and weeds.

It is important to buy quality. A little extra money invested can guarantee longer life and better durability. Cheap bargain or inexpensive tools often do not stand the test of time. So in this case, the saying 'you get what you pay for' is very true.

Think carefully when buying tools. Electric mowers, cultivators, hedge trimmers and other aides need less maintenance than their fuel-powered counterparts. They do not suffer from starting problems and are also lighter to handle. Finance permitting, choose a mower with a wide cut as this reduces mowing time considerably. Also, choose one that collects the grass rather than leaving it for you to rake up afterwards. Two-wheel barrows are lighter on the arms than single-wheel models. If you prefer a single-wheel model, one with a pneumatic tyre will be easier to push on uneven ground. Tools with quick-change heads that fit onto a single handle are convenient and save you carrying an armful of equipment. Nylon cord trimmers make light work of grass trimming and will cut right up to trees and fences.

Checklist

- Spade
- Fork
- Trowel
- Hand fork
- Rake
- Hoe
- Shears
- Secateurs
- Wheelbarrow
- Lawnmower

Old-style metal wheelbarrow in the herb garden at Ballymaloe

Storage and Care

Your garden tools will last much longer if you take good care of them. It is very important they are always kept clean and stored in a dry place. Position them somewhere where they are readily accessible. Hanging your garden tools in a shed or garage may help to keep them out of reach of children and prevent accidents occurring. If you have ever stepped on the head of a rake you'll know exactly what I mean! Before putting spades and forks away, you must remove and scrape away any soil. I use an old kitchen fork for the job and, once cleaned, I give the tools a good rub with an oily rag.

Tip

Keep an old bucket handy. This should be filled with coarse or sharp sand. Even grit will do. Add to this some diesel oil. This mixture will allow you to clean tools conveniently by inserting the spade or fork up and down in the mixture. You are removing dirt and, at the same time, coating it with a protective layer of oil.

Power Tools

For many, spring brings power tools out of storage and into use in the garden. Safety is of paramount importance when it comes to using electric garden equipment. It is imperative that you take great care to read and then carry out all the safety instructions which are provided by the manufacturer's handbooks with these tools. You should never, ever, take any risks.

● With electrical equipment, always use a circuit breaker. This will prevent electric shock if the cable is accidentally cut. For the small price you pay for this device, you could save a lot of pain and injury.

● Before cleaning or unblocking any electrical equipment, disconnect from the main power supply.

● Many machines contain safety guards. These must never be removed. A finger or a toe can be lost too easily.

● Make sure to wear the appropriate and recommended safety clothing – goggles and gloves, safety helmets, ear protection and, if necessary, steel-tipped shoes.

Each year, hospitals witness a large number of casualties as the result of garden accidents. If simple safety guidelines are followed, these accidents can be avoided.

Rubber-tyred wheelbarrow – good for uneven surfaces

Hints

Stainless steel is best

For the ultimate in ease and pleasure of use, combined with simplicity of maintenance, choose stainless steel garden tools.

Choose your weight

Never buy a garden tool of any type until you have had the chance to handle it. Weight and balance are very important criteria and can only be judged by each individual gardener.

Essential items

If you don't want, or can't afford, a complete set of garden tools, your priority purchases should be: border fork, border spade, weeding fork, trowel, spring-tine rake and a Dutch or similar hoe.

Safe shear sharpening

Don't be tempted to try sharpening high quality secateurs or shears yourself – have the job done professionally.

Care for your secateurs

After pruning, clean the resinous sap from secateurs, and disinfect them at the same time by wiping them thoroughly with a cloth soaked in meths or alcohol.

Which wheelbarrow?

If you have large areas of fairly soft ground in your garden or have to push your wheelbarrow across the lawn fairly frequently, why not choose one with a ball-pattern wheel? These are remarkably easy to push and won't compact the ground.

Compatible hoses

When buying hose accessories, it makes sense to stick to the products of one of the major manufacturers for you may find that not all equipment is compatible and you could end up with annoying leaks.

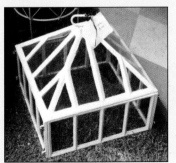

Victorian cloche

Pyrus salicifolia 'Pendula' – commonly known as the weeping silver pear. A beautiful tree suited to the smaller garden

Trees

Choosing the Right Tree

Trees can be a delight or a disaster. Choosing the right tree is only part of the story. Where you put it is almost as critical. Unless you have a very small garden you may find that it is more effective to plant several trees rather than rely on one specimen as a focal point. Firstly, you should decide what you want from a tree. Is it shade, shelter from wind, or simply something beautiful to look at? For shade, you will need a relatively tall tree with spreading branches. For shelter, you will need upright conifers or other trees that extend their foliage to ground level. But if you are looking for a tree to enhance your garden you will find that the choice is vast. You can choose from trees with stunning autumn foliage, enchanting spring blossoms, attractive bark or delicate summer foliage. You must also decide whether you want a tree to be deciduous or evergreen. You can enjoy the changing seasons as a tree can give you year-round interest. The eventual height and spread must always be taken into consideration and whether the tree is a fast or slow grower. Always allow for the extent of shade your tree will cast, especially if there is a rock garden or pool. You must also consider whether the

Magnolia x soulangeana 'Alba'

shade will affect your neighbours. Some tree roots can affect and damage drains and foundations so plant any tree well away from the house. You should be especially careful when planting trees such as willows. When thinking about the best tree for your garden, it may be useful to visit gardens open to the public, taking note of trees you may like and paying special attention to their height and spread. Visit a reputable garden centre where you can seek advice from qualified staff. All of this will help you make the right choice.

Buying the Tree

Small young trees are the best buys. They become established more quickly than larger ones and, in many cases, they even catch up with them within 2-3 years. If you are buying bare-rooted trees with or without some surrounding soil make sure to satisfy yourself that they have a well-developed root system. If the trees are not bare-rooted look for sturdy, close-jointed shoots and a strong stem.

Betula utilis var. jacquemontii – a superb birch noted for its exceptional white bark which is best appreciated through the winter months

Soil Preparation

It is very important to bear in mind a tree's long life span. It is worth going to that extra trouble to ensure that the soil is in good condition before planting. The difference this makes is tremendous to the quality and life of the tree. Make sure that the soil is well-drained and that you have dug in plenty of organic matter, for example farmyard manure or well-rotted compost. Dig an area of soil up to twice the width of the tree's root span and 10-12in deep.

Place the soil to once side. With a fork, break up and loose the subsoil in the bottom of the planting hole. Now mix the well-rotted manure or garden compost with the soil removed from the hole. Add some slow-release fertiliser and your mix is ready for planting.

Planting

The tree should be planted at the same depth as the one in which it had been previously growing, whether it is in open ground or in a container. Hold the tree upright in the planting hole and place a stick across the hole at ground level. Check that the line of the stick corresponds with the soil mark on the stem. This is especially important if the tree is bare-rooted. Otherwise, make sure that it is at the level of the container. Add or remove soil from the base of the soil to adjust the tree's height as necessary. Hammer in a stake just a little from the centre of the hole. Hold the tree in place again, with its stem close to the stake and shovel in the prepared soil, between and over the roots. When they are partially covered, shake the tree gently to eliminate any air pockets. Continue firming the soil by treading it until the hole is filled. Finally, secure the tree to the stake and give the ground a good soaking, especially if the soil is dry.

Supporting

There are two reasons for supporting a young tree. One is to prevent it being blown over at an angle by the wind and the other is to avoid wind rock, which prevents the roots from securing a firm hold. Except on very exposed sites, staking is only necessary for the first 2-3 years. A short stake can be used as this allows some movement in the top of the tree, which encourages and stimulates extra root development. Use a single tie, fastening the tree to the stake. It is important not to let the stem of the tree rub against the stake. You will need to check the tie at regular intervals to make sure that it has not worked loose or is not pressing too tightly on the stem. Specially designed tree straps are available from garden centres.

Trunks of newly planted trees can be protected from animal damage by using a plastic guard which wraps in a spiral around the trunk.

Trees for Small Gardens

Prunus (Ornamental Cherry)
Height: Variable
Spread: Variable

There are many different forms ranging in height and spread. If you're looking for one suitable for a small garden it's essential to seek expert advice. I would recommend Prunus amanogaua, which grows as a tall, narrow column and produces beautiful pale pink cherry blossoms in spring.

Acer palmatum 'Dissectum'
Height: 8-10ft
Spread: 10ft

Beautiful foliage which provides a marvellous autumn colour. Will grow in sun or shade.

Malus (Crab Apple)
Height: Up to 15ft
Spread: Up to 12ft

There are many different types which are grown for their spring flowers and crab apples which appear later. Will grow in sun or light shade. It is worthwhile visiting a garden centre to see what varieties are available.

Crataegus (Hawthorn)
Height: 15ft approx
Spread: 15ft approx

There are several forms with either white, pink or red flowers and in autumn they produce scarlet haws. It will grow in sun or light shade.

Juniperus virginiana 'Sky Rocket'
Height: 12ft approx
Spread: 24in approx

This grows to a height of approximately 12ft with a spread of approximately 24in. It makes a tall slender evergreen and is a grey-blue leafed conifer. It will grow in sun or light shade.

Ornamental cherry blossom

Hints

Weed-free zone

Always keep an area about 1m (3ft) in diameter close to a newly planted young tree free from weeds. Although the tree will be robust enough when mature, it is no more capable of competing effectively with weed growth than any other small plant.

Honey fungus

After cutting down a deciduous tree, try to remove the stump or have it ground out. At the very least, cover it with soil as the cut surface can provide an entry point for honey fungus to establish itself in your garden.

Trees and the law

You are perfectly entitled to cut branches off a neighbour's tree that overhangs your garden; but legally you are obliged to offer him the material that you cut off.

Safe ties

When attaching a belt-style tie to secure a tree to a stake, be sure to fix the buckle adjacent to the stake, not to the tree, which will be damaged by it. Check the ties on fast-growing trees and shrubs at least once a year – rapid growth in girth can result in the plant strangling itself.

When using wire to tie up or support the branches of trees or large shrubs, slip a short length of old hosepipe over the wire where it is in contact with the branch to prevent damage.

Japanese maples

Do not plant ornamental Japanese maples in a position where they will be subjected to water logged soil or strong winds.

Keep poplars away from apples

Never plant poplars as windbreaks round apple orchards as they can harbour canker disease.

Acer griseum (the paper bark maple) an easy to grow tree which reveals its peeling cinnamon-coloured bark in winter

Care Calendar

January
Check the ties on young trees to ensure that stems are not being damaged.

February
Remove low branches from established trees if necessary.

March
Plant bare-rooted evergreen trees.

April
Make sure to control weeds growing over the root zone of young trees.

May
Check all trees planted in the past year for signs of drought.

June
Trees in pots can be planted now, but it's essential to water on a regular basis.

July
Check older trees for signs that tree ties are not choking or cutting into stems.

August
Continue to check that newly planted trees are not suffering from drought.

September
Dig the ground thoroughly in preparation for the planting of trees later on. Order trees from your local garden centre for planting this autumn.

October
Start planting evergreens – preferably during showery weather.

November
Towards the end of this month, begin planting hardy deciduous trees in well prepared ground. Use stakes to support young trees until they are established.

December
Provide wind breaks for newly planted evergreens while they are establishing.

Cornus controversa 'Variegata'

Hydrangea macrophylla 'La France'

Shrubs

When you visit a garden centre you will be amazed at the bewildering range of shrubs that are available. The choice is fantastic. You will be able to select everything from evergreen to deciduous, flowering to berrying, brightly coloured foliage from upright to spreading, from wide-growing to thin. Whatever you need for your garden there is a shrub to fill the gap.

Magnolia stellata (Star Magnolia)

Shrubs for Shade

One of the most difficult places to grow shrubs in your garden is in a dry shady spot under trees. For this difficult spot, ivy is an excellent choice as a ground cover. You could also try vinca or pachysandra. All are evergreen and, once helped to establish into these conditions, will grow extremely well. Autumn is probably the best time to plant shrubs under trees, but the job can also be done in early spring. The soil can be too dry in summer and there is a greater risk of plants

Paeonia x lemoinea 'Souvenir de Maxime Cornu'

drying out and not establishing. If you are looking for taller plants it is absolutely essential that you water these well for the first few seasons while they are establishing, working their own roots into the soil. Here are five shrubs which are ideal for this difficult position:

1. Mahonia
These produce strong evergreen foliage and most have sweetly scented yellow flowers in winter.

2. Aucuba japonica
A shrub with rich, glossy foliage. The variegated form is covered with golden yellow spots. It is very effective at brightening up a shaded area.

With female plants you also have the bonus of berries.

3. Euonymous fortunei
The variegated form is very handsome and looks particularly bright when the new leaves are developing in spring.

4. Buxus sempervirens
Commonly known as box. Once established this plant is easy to grow and can be clipped into shapes. The variegated forms with brighter foliage are occasionally available.

5. Ilex aquifolium (Holly)
Commonly known as holly, all varieties are excellent in shade. There are some splendid silver and golden variegated forms available. To have berries, in the majority of cases, you will need male and female plants.

Tree Lupin
This is an old-fashioned shrub, easy to grow and very suited to sheltered coastal sites. The usual colour is yellow, but sometimes it can be seen in blue or mauve. It enjoys free-draining soil and it will be necessary to keep an eye out for greenfly early in the season. It can be grown from cuttings or from seed.

Lupinus arboreus (Tree Lupin)

Chaenomeles x superba 'Rowallane'

Chaenomeles

A very valuable early-flowering shrub, available in red, white or pink. The red crimson types provide a valuable splash of colour early in the season. Not difficult to grow and long-lived.

Protect newly planted evergreen shrubs from strong winds. Using a windbreak to filter wind will assist plants in establishing and prevent wind dehydrating them, causing scorch and even death.

Evergreen shrubs supplied with a wrapped ball of soil known as a rootball are best planted in spring or in autumn, not during the winter. Try to keep this ball of soil intact when planting and make sure it does not dry out.

Make sure that spring planted shrubs are not allowed to dry out. The majority of newly planted shrubs that die usually do so as a result of drought.

Suckers growing from beneath the ground alongside grafted shrubs should be pulled away from the rootstock.

Sparse flowering may be the result of overfeeding, especially if the plant is naturally vigorous. In average soil, shrubs should be able to find all the nutrients they need without too much artificial feeding. But of course, shrubs grown in containers are an exception.

Ceanothus 'Concha'

Philadelphus 'Belle Etoile'

Acer palmatum atropurpureum dissectum 'Garnet'

Foliar Feeding

Spraying a shrub with liquid fertiliser will give it a boost during prolonged dry weather when the roots are unable to take up sufficient nutrients.

Ceanothus

These are among the most beautiful blue-flowered shrubs of late spring and early summer. They are evergreen and, when in full flower, they cover themselves in blue blossom from top to bottom.

Philadelphus

If you are looking for a shrub with attractive flowers and a really rich scent, Philadelphus is a must. This is a deciduous shrub that is happy in a sunny position growing in most soils. It can also be grown against a wall and in early summer the white flowers will fill your garden with the sweetest fragrance.

Tree Peonies

Tree peonies make magnificent shrubs. They need to be planted in a sheltered place where their new spring foliage is protected from wind. They enjoy sun and rich, well-drained soil. They are long-lived and when in full flower provide magnificent flowers in a wide range of colours.

Pruning

Many shrubs need little or no pruning from one year to another. Others will flower more freely and maintain a better shape if pruned on an annual basis. When and how this is done varies from plant to plant. The crucial point in many cases is where the flowers are carried on the previous year's growth or the shoots that have formed during the current season. Make all pruning cuts immediately above an outward-facing bud. Remove dead and diseased shoots and any that are weak or misplaced, even if overall pruning is unnecessary. When pruning on the previous season's growth, do this immediately after flowering, cutting the shoots that have flowered back to the new wood. This will encourage fresh shoots which will carry the following year's flowers. Early spring is the time to prune shrubs that flower on the current season's

Paeonia 'Duchesse de Morny' (Tree Peony)

• After flowering, cut back shrubs that flower on last year's shoots, for example forsythia. New growth will form to carry next year's flowers.

• Fairly heavy spring pruning will induce better flowers on shrubs that bloom on the current year's growth, for example roses.

• Remove some of the older branches from neglected shrubs and, if necessary, cut them back to ground level.

Buying

When buying container grown shrubs, check that no large roots are protruding and that there is no gap between the compost and the

shoots, for example buddleia. Cut back last year's shoots to within about three buds of their base. Neglected, overcrowded shrubs can often be rejuvenated by cutting out old branches at the base. This will leave more space for younger growth to emerge. This is much more effective than simply shortening the branches which will cause an even denser growth. After hard pruning of this sort, give the shrub a dressing of general fertiliser around the root area and an application or mulch of well-rotted manure will also help.

• With all types of shrubs, the first step is to cut out any weak growth, diseased or dead shoots.

Paeonia rockii (Tree Peony)

Melianthus major

plastic of the pot. If you are buying shrubs during spring or summer it is important to check that the leaves and shoots are healthy and pest free. In autumn and winter bare-root plants should have plenty of strong roots and be fully dormant when you are buying them. Always select plants which have sturdy, well-placed stems.

Soil Preparation

When you are planting, your main aim is to provide the conditions that will encourage a good root system to develop. Root development can easily be hampered if the surrounding soil is either excessively wet or dry. If you are planting a shrub in normal soil,

the ground should be dug some weeks before planting and well-rotted manure or garden compost should be incorporated at the same time.

Planting

Plant a container-grown shrub by digging an oversized planting hole. Make sure when positioning the plant and refilling that the soil going back into the hole is firmed well. It is useful to sprinkle an application of slow-release fertiliser which can be mixed through the soil which is refilling the planting hole.

If you purchase a bare-root shrub in the dormant season and you are not ready to plant it straight away, remove the packaging and heel it into the ground temporarily. This means digging a hole or a trench big enough to take the roots which then need to be covered with soil. This prevents the roots drying out and becoming dehydrated.

Buddleja davidii 'Nanho Petite Indigo'

Care Calendar

January

Move established shrubs that are in the wrong place.

February

This is a good month to look out for winter-flowering shrubs for your garden.

March

Make sure that newly-planted shrubs receive water during dry spells.

April

Cut back dogwoods to encourage new growth for next winter's bark effect.

May

Make sure that camellias receive sequestered iron.

June

Early-flowering shrubs that have finished flowering can be pruned this month.

July

Hydrangeas need constant watering if flowers are to develop well.

August

Take semi-hardwood cuttings of many kinds of shrubs including fuchsia, philadelphus and escallonia.

September

Lightly clip evergreens, but not in exposed areas.

October

This is a good month for planting new shrubs.

November

Make sure that soil is well prepared and continue to plant.

December

Visit garden centres. This is a good time to buy specimen shrubs as a wider selection is available at this time.

Weeping Japanese maple overhanging a pool

A collection of David Austin roses surrounded by box hedging. These roses have been bred using a combination of old-fashioned and modern types retaining the best characteristics of both

Roses

I could never imagine having a garden without roses. They have always been among my favourite plants. I enjoy them for many reasons, primarily the colour and fragrance that they bring to the garden. I also believe that they offer fantastic value and you can generally have them in flower from May until October. By following a few simple guidelines, they are easy to care for and the selection and variety available today guarantees a rose for every situation.

Types of Roses

Hybrid Tea Roses

Hybrid tea roses bear large flowers. They have many petals and are recognisable by a single central cone. The flowers are borne singly or with several side buds. Hybrid teas are among the most popular and widely available roses and are available as either bush or standard.

Rambling Rose 'Albertine' – noted for its beautiful fragrance

Floribunda

In popularity, Floribundas come second only to the hybrid tea. They are recognisable as their flowers are borne in clusters or trusses with many flowers opening together. They give a magnificent display and are perfect roses for a good splash of colour where it's needed.

Climbing and Rambling

Climbing roses have stiff upright stems and usually bear flowers which are much larger than rambling types. They also are more inclined to provide a repeat display of flowers. Ramblers bear large trusses of flowers, usually small in size. These commonly appear as a once-off summer flush. Their

Rosa 'Arkle' (Hybrid Tea)

Rosa 'Henry Martin' (Moss Rose)

From autumn into early winter, many garden centres stock bare-root roses. These have been lifted from the ground and their roots wrapped to protect from dehydration. The roses are dormant and can be planted, weather-permitting, any time up to mid-March.

At any other time of year, roses can be purchased container grown. This prevents disturbance of growing roots and allows you a longer planting period. Container-grown roses are usually available from the beginning of March until mid-summer.

Occasionally, you may come across pre-packaged roses. These are usually offered in supermarkets. It is important to check that these roses have not started into growth. They are best planted during the dormant period, from

growth is longer and is inclined to spread more, creating a rambling habit. Support is needed for both.

Shrub Roses

Shrub roses are much larger than hybrid teas and floribundas in their growth. There are many different groups which come under this category, old-fashioned and modern being two. They are generally easy-care and usually provide one flush of flowers in the summer. There are also some wonderful species roses, which make superb flowering shrubs for your garden.

Buying Roses

When buying a rose the secret is to purchase early in the gardening season. You will find there is a greater selection available in garden centres at this time.

Rosa 'Charles de Mills' (Shrub Rose)

November to early March. If kept too warm, dehydration, premature growth, and shrivelling can occur, rendering the rose useless.

When buying a rose, quality is all-important. I recommend you purchase from a reliable source. This way, you are guaranteed true-to-name varieties and excellent young plants, which get the very best start.

Planting

Bare-root roses should be planted for best results between the end of October until the end of March. Container-grown plants can be planted at any time of year, providing the weather and soil conditions are suitable. Best

Rosa 'Tuscany' – synonym: 'Old Velvet Rose'

results, though, are achieved by planting in either spring or autumn.

Soil preparation is all-important. Once you have planted your rose, you will expect many years of pleasure and enjoyment from it. A little time and effort spent on preparing the soil is setting up the right conditions to guarantee you a healthy and beautiful plant for as long as possible. Dig the soil well in advance and incorporate organic matter, for example, well-rotted manure. This will help to enrich the soil, improving its texture and quality and will also provide necessary nutrients for the new rose.

Position your roses in full sun. This will encourage extra flowers and a strong, healthy-growing plant. Avoid soil where there are extremes of either wet or drought. Roses enjoy average moisture and, in very dry spells, may require additional watering.

David Austin *Rosa* 'Benjamin Britten', a new English Rose

Care

Pruning

Traditionally, St. Patrick's Day has always been the time when Irish gardeners pruned their roses. It is important to use a sharp secateurs as this will give a clean cut preventing disease entering the wound. It also means you are less likely to crush the stem. Make the cut approximately half a centimetre above a bud. Ideally this should be slightly sloping away to the back but not sloping below the bud itself. If possible, you should avoid leaving long snags above a bud as these will die back sometimes carrying dead growth down behind the bud which may damage new growth. When pruning you should cut out all dead and diseased growth. Also, cut back all of last year's growth to between two and four buds above the ground. Try to select outward-facing buds. This will encourage a more pleasing shape and helps avoid tangled stems. With climbing roses you will need to

Rosa 'Belvedere' – rambling rose

Rosa 'Graham Thomas'

remove any stems growing in the wrong direction, but rather than cutting hard to the ground you will need to tidy the plant back to the wall.

Dead-heading

Dead-heading roses is very important and by carrying out this practice you can guarantee yourself extra flowers. By removing the dead flowers, you are preventing energy going into developing seedheads. When the flowers have faded, cut the stem 3-4 leaves below the flower. This will ensure a new flowering shoot, which will bring you extra colour a little later. There is no need to remove dead flowers on roses which are grown for their decorative hips or roses which are only once-flowering.

Feeding

Roses provide a fantastic display and offer superb value for money. But to get the very best from your rose and to guarantee a healthy show of flowers, it is essential that you feed on a regular basis. Rose blossoms make a great demand on the plant and so supplementing with feeding ensures a good crop.

The most popular rose feeds, which are widely available, are granular fertilisers. These contain a special blend of nutrients, including magnesium, which is very important to roses. This blend is specially formulated to give the rose everything it needs to perform well. These granular feeds should only be used while the rose is in active growth. They do not contribute to improving the soil but act quickly by feeding the rose.

Rosa 'Albertine' (Rambler)

Rosa 'Mundi' (Gallica)

Liquid fertilisers are also available. These are an excellent choice for quick feeding. It is advisable to feed on a regular basis, following instructions. It is best to use little and often rather than apply one strong application.

To improve the quality of soil and feed at the same time, it is a good idea to apply a mulch of well-rotted manure. This can be purchased pre-packed in garden centres. It is most beneficial when applied in autumn, allowing the winter weather time to work on it.

Pests and Disease Control

Greenfly

The most common pest on roses is the greenfly (aphid). This is the most serious pest and is inclined to attack new developing growth and if left unchecked will cause stunting and distortion of new leaves and of developing flowers. The best way to deal with this pest is to use a systemic insecticide or one of the many organic greenfly sprays available. It is important to keep a close eye in spring on new growth as it starts to develop. Treatment may be necessary once a fortnight. It is important not to spray roses in very bright sunlight as this can cause damage to soft new growth. It is essential that you follow instructions when preparing sprays. It is also important that you wear protective clothing and avoid spraying in windy conditions.

Rosa 'Lady Hillingdon' (Climbing)

Rosa 'Königin von Dänemark' (Queen of Denmark) (Alba)

Rosa 'Albertine' with a bad attack of blackspot

Diseases

Blackspot

Blackspot is one of the most common disease problems with roses. It is encouraged by warm, wet summers and is also encouraged by a shortage of potassium. It can be difficult to control. It is necessary in bad cases to remove leaves and destroy them by burning. Use a systemic fungicide once a fortnight from when the leaves first start to appear in early spring.

An organic method which is inexpensive and effective if used on a regular basis is detailed below.

Dermot's Blackspot and Mildew Remedy

Dissolve three heaped teaspoons of Bicarbonate of Soda (Baking Powder) in a small amount of water. Add a small dash of washing-up liquid. Add this mixture to a watering can containing one gallon of water. Using a rose on the watering can, wet the foliage thoroughly, but not during hours of direct sunlight. This can be applied once a fortnight and will also control mildew.

Mildew

Mildew is one of the most widespread of fungal diseases. It appears as a white powdery mould and is clearly visible on new leaves and buds. It is most prevalent in summer and damp days of early autumn. It can be encouraged by dryness at the root and by warm days followed by cold nights. Use a systemic fungicide or Dermot's Blackspot and Mildew Remedy.

Rust

Rust is a more unusual disease which can affect roses. It generally occurs if there is a deficiency of potassium or if a dry, warm summer has followed a cold spring.

Rosa 'Alnwick Castle' (David Austin)

Rosa 'Intrigue'

Dermot picks the best roses for your garden

Over many years, I have grown a great number of roses. Many of them are now like old friends greeting me each year as they come into flower. Selecting favourite roses is very much a personal choice and with such a huge range from which to choose, I feel it is important to select those that have been tried and tested. Here are roses which offer that something extra setting them apart, making them special roses to grow.

It appears as rust-coloured or orange swellings on the underside of foliage. These usually turn black in late summer. The usual time of appearance is July and it is necessary to use a systemic fungicide as this disease can be fatal if not checked.

To keep your roses pest and disease free it is useful to follow a spray programme. Use a systemic insecticide and fungicide, spraying in mid-May, mid-June and early September. You can use extra spray treatments if the need arises, but generally these three main applications will keep your roses healthy and looking good.

Rosa 'Buff Beauty'

Rosa 'Rhapsody in Blue'

spectacular rose and it is sad that it's not widely available.

Madame Caroline Testout

When in full flower climbing 'Madame Caroline Testout' is covered in enormous silvery, satin pink blouse blooms which are exquisitely rolled and ruffled around the edges.

This climbing rose was named after a late 19th century French couturiére from Grenoble. She was the proprietress of the most fashionable salons of the day in Paris and London. Madame

Rhapsody in Blue

This rose won the Rose of the Year Award for 2003 and has created great excitement around the world for its unusual colouring. The flowers open purple-tinted and fade to slate blue tones. This is the nearest to blue that rose breeders have so far managed to produce. It is tall and bushy and is continuous flowering. It has a sweet scent.

Souvenir de Georges Pernet

An extremely rare and strong-growing climbing rose which has practically vanished from cultivation. It was first introduced in 1927 and is noted for its exceptional vigour and extremely double large flowers, each having forty petals. It is a climbing rose that requires full sun and can grow over 10ft in height. It is lightly scented. It is a

Rosa 'Souvenir de Georges Pernet'

Rosa 'Souvenir de St Anne's'

chance natural crossing of a China rose Old Blush with a Damask rose Quatre Saisons resulted in the start of a new race of roses collectively known as the Bourbons. The next two roses belong to this group. The first is 'Souvenir de St Anne's', named after Lord and Lady Ardilaun's famous garden at Clontarf in Dublin. Today it's one of Europe's greatest rose gardens, lovingly cared for by Dublin Corporation and well worth a visit during the summer.

Souvenir de St Anne's

'Souvenir de St Anne's' was discovered growing as a sport on a bush of another celebrated rose, Souvenir de la Malmaison. It was spotted by the head gardener, who had a keen eye for good plants. The rose was a great treasure of the garden and was watchfully guarded and protected by Lady Ardilaun, who was very reluctant to part with one of her treasures, but did so on condition that it was to be kept only by the recipient. In time a plant was passed on to Lady Moore, wife of Sir Frederick Moore, Director of the Botanic Gardens, Glasnevin. Lady Moore was a renowned Irish gardener who grew the rose at Willbrook, Rathfarnham, Co. Dublin. In the early 1950s Lady Moore gave the rose to Graham Thomas, and thanks to her this special Irish rose can be grown by you today. It grows to about a metre and a half in height and provides fragrant blossoms from May until early August. The semidouble blossoms are the colour of rich pink pearls, a beautiful shell pink colour that softly blends into cream.

Testout travelled extensively to purchase fabrics for her wealthy clients, and on one such trip to Lyons – famous for silk production – she heard tell of a talented rose breeder, Joseph Pernet-Ducher, who was developing the latest rage of the time, 'Hybrid Teas'. A meeting was arranged, and after much negotiation she persuaded Monsieur Pernet-Ducher to name a rose of his choice after her. In the spring of 1890 the new rose made its premiere at the salon's fashion shows in London and Paris. The rose was an instant success and was all the rage with her rich and famous clients.

Now over one hundred years on, there are few rivals, even from some very fine modern creations. This rose in full bloom is a startling spectacle.

In 1817 on Isle de Bourbon, an island in the South Indian Ocean today known as Reunion, a

Madame Isaac Pereire

The next Bourbon rose ranks highly among the most richly fragrant of all roses, 'Madame Isaac Pereire'. I can only describe its fragrance as exquisitely sumptuous, reminiscent of a bowl of freshly picked sweet raspberries. The flowers are an example of full petalled perfection, enormous and cup-shaped. The colour is deep carmine pink, beautifully clouded with magenta. The first flush is in June and is followed in autumn by an even better display. I think Madame Isaac Pereire likes the cool damp air of autumn. This rose will make a strong bush, but is equally good as a climber.

Dainty Bess

Now for something completely different, an outstanding variety from the 1920s which evokes much of the spirit of that era. 'Dainty Bess' is my favourite single hybrid tea. In full flower it is irresistible and supremely beautiful. The flowers start as shapely pointed buds and open to single five-petal flowers of a light silvery pink. The underside of each petal is soft carmine and the centre of the rose is crowned with a ring of purple/brown stamens. The overall effect is unbeatably refined.

The colour is delicate and soothing, reminding one of the colours you find in shell striped brocades and floral cottons. The flowers are borne singly or in clusters through out the summer. It is ideally suited to the small garden, growing only about three feet high.

Just Joey

In 1994 the Hybrid Tea 'Just Joey' was voted the world's favourite rose. Firstly I must tell you that Just Joey is perfectly suited to Irish weather conditions as the flowers stand up very well to all our rainy weather. The large flowers are a remarkable colour combination; copper, orange, pink fading to creamy orange. As the flower matures you will find the blush oranges you see inside seashells with the mellow glow of a Mediterranean sunset. Each petal has a beautiful wavy edge, set off by a deep purple toned leaf - the combination is

Rosa 'Dainty Bess'

Rosa 'James Galway'

James Galway

Named to celebrate the 60th birthday of world-famous flautist James Galway. This rose can be grown as a bushy shrub and also makes an excellent low-growing climber. The flowers are large and full and the colour is a beautiful warm pink at the centre fading to pale pink at the edges. It has a delicious old-rose fragrance and the stems are almost thornless, adding to its appeal as a climber.

Trumpeter

Like me, you will appreciate a rose which is largely trouble-free and flowers dependably throughout the summer. This is the case for 'Trumpeter', a low-growing rose no more than two foot high, but what a performer! This bush produces a lavish display of abundant clusters, vibrant bright ruby red to crimson flowers, a sensational effect. I think red is the colour in the spectrum which draws the eye the most. Trumpeter does just that, and looks fantastic if grown in a container - portable colour which will add a blast of intensity to any part of your garden. If grown with purples or rich blues the contrast will be entrancing.

White Flower Carpet

This is a marvellous rose for ground cover. It is low growing and spreads. Starting to flower in May and continuing into autumn, it provides excellent value. Flower carpet roses come in a range of colours including red, yellow, salmon and pink. They are generally disease resistant and will guarantee you a colourful display for a long period.

memorable. It also makes a beautiful cut flower and it is widely available. Do try it.

Iceberg

The best white Floribunda you can grow has got to be 'Iceberg'. There have been many contenders for its throne but none have withstood the test of time. When I think of this outstanding white rose I think of the soft translucence of marble, the purity of its cool calm colour and the wonderful summer display it gives. Iceberg can be used with practically any other plant, its white flowers always adding a look of freshness, giving lift and spirit to the garden. Iceberg makes an impressive specimen growing to about four feet high. It also looks good as a standard making an impressive centrepiece. Underplant this rose with a viola 'Molly Sanderson', which has pure coal black flowers. The contrast will impress.

Sexy Rexy

One of the very best soft-pink floribundas. This rose grows approximately 3-4ft in height and puts on a stunning display from mid to late summer. It is generally disease resistant and is always admired when seen growing with the lavender blue of catmint.

Pierre de Ronsard

This is a strong-growing climbing rose which was bred in 1987 by Meilland of France. It has gorgeous flowers which are of old-fashioned style. They are very full and cabbage in shape. The base colour is creamy white which is heavily suffused with pink and carmine. It repeat flowers throughout the summer into autumn and has a pleasant light fragrance. It is named after a court poet who lived in Scotland between 1524 and 1585.

Rosa 'Pierre de Ronsard'

Graham Thomas

Graham Thomas belongs to a group of roses called 'English Roses'. This was bred by the famous rose breeder David Austin in 1983. It was named to honour the leading authority on old-fashioned roses and has become one of the all-time best selling modern shrub roses today. It is a fantastic and spectacular rose when in full flower. The flowers are large double and a deep yellow in colour. The yellow you will find in the egg yolk of a free range egg. The foliage is dark green. It grows 3-4ft in height and when in flower has a slightly arching habit. It repeat flowers throughout the summer and each flower has a beautiful tea-like fragrance.

Rosa 'Graham Thomas'

Climbing rose 'Sympathie'

Hints

Replant disease

When replanting an old rose bed with new stock, there is always a risk of the plants failing to establish satisfactorily because of rose replant disease. Either leave the soil free from roses for two years or dig out a hole of about 30cm (1ft) cube for each plant and refill it with soil taken from another part of the garden.

Painless roses

If you want a climbing rose close to a doorway or path, and you are worried about the prickles, grow the thornless climber 'Zephirine Drouhin'.

How to avoid suckers

To avoid the problem of rose suckers, take cuttings from your plants in late autumn. Use 25 cm (10in) lengths of woody shoots of the current year's growth and insert them 15cm (6in) deep in a shady corner of the garden. The resulting bushes

will be growing on their own roots and all shoots will therefore be of the flowering variety.

Pegging climbers

Bend and peg the shoots of climbing roses down to slightly below the horizontal to encourage flowering along their entire length.

How to dead-head

When dead-heading roses, cut the stem back to a point just above the first leaf bearing five, not three, leaflets.

Wet weather problem

Don't be unduly concerned if the flowers on some of your roses fail to open properly in very wet weather. This is a condition called balling and is an unavoidable problem on some thinner-petalled varieties. It seems to affect many very old-fashioned varieties that are very double, carrying a lot of extra petals.

Protecting roses from wind damage

All types of roses are likely to produce a few abnormally long shoots and even if these are required to form part of the plant's permanent framework, they should be shortened by about a third and, if necessary, tied in, in the late autumn before they are whipped around by winter winds.
Rose bushes are rather prone to being moved around in the ground by the wind, so creating a small hollow at the base of the stem. This should be filled in with soil and the plant carefully firmed. Otherwise, rainwater will collect in the hollow and then freeze, so causing damage to the stem tissues.

Care Calendar

January

There is little to do with roses this month as frosts are likely. This is a good time to order roses from specialist rose companies who can provide some of the more unusual types.

February

Weather permitting, and if the soil is not too wet, you can continue to plant roses. It is important that temperatures are above freezing.

March

Finish planting roses and if you have not already pruned, the job should be carried out by St. Patrick's Day. Fertiliser can be sprinkled around roses after pruning.

April

It is essential that pruning is completed by now. You can sprinkle a granular fertiliser.

May

Keep an eye that weeds do not develop as they will cause competition. Do not dig around your roses. Weeding should be carried out by hand. It is important to keep an eye out for greenfly as attack is most likely this month. You can use a liquid feed on your roses this month.

June

Weeding, watering, spraying will all need to be carried out this month. Insecticides and fungicides can be used to keep problems at bay.

July

Dead-head and apply a summer dressing of granular fertiliser. Continue to pay attention to weeds and it may be necessary to apply a mulch. This is a good month to visit a garden centre and admire roses, taking note of varieties you may wish to plant in autumn.

August

Feeding should have stopped by now. Continue keeping a close eye for pests and diseases and treat if necessary.

September

It is important to continue dead-heading as this helps to guarantee the flowering of your roses for as long as possible. Summer flowering roses can now be pruned. Continue dealing with weeds and dealing with pests and diseases.

October

Hygiene is very important during this month. Remove and burn fallen leaves. Keep the rose bed tidy. Prepare new areas for planting.

November

Planting of bare-root roses can be carried out now. It is important to heal these in if you are not ready for the planting job. This will prevent roots dehydrating.

December

Weather conditions will be getting wetter so carry out planting before the end of the month. Avoid planting if weather is frosty or the ground is too wet.

Wisteria sinensis trained along a bridge

Climbing Plants

Make the most of climbing plants by adding a vertical dimension to your garden or simply camouflage an eyesore. Climbing plants are an essential feature of every garden and they can be used to transform a wall, trellis or fence. Alternatively, you can grow climbing plants through other plants, especially shrub varieties that flower early in the season. A climbing plant can add that extra colour later in the year.

As well as growing, climbing plants simply for the flowers, berries or autumn colour, you can use them to disguise an unsightly oil tank, to screen dustbins or to conceal some other unattractive feature.

Planting

Climbing plants will grow for many years so it is essential to prepare the soil well before planting. Dig organic matter deeply into the surrounding soil. Dig the hole deeper and wider than necessary and break up the bottom of the hole. Add some organic matter and lightly fork it into the bottom.

When planting close to a wall it is necessary that the plant is at least 12in away from it, or even a little more. This is because the soil at the base of a wall is often very dry. For the same reason, if you are growing the plant through a bush or tree, plant it away from the trunk. When planting a climber,

Tropaeolum speciosum (Flame Flower). The brilliant scarlet flowers stand out against the dark foliage of a yew hedge

make certain that the level of the soil around the plant stem is the same as it was when the plant was in its container. An exception to this rule is clematis, which should always be planted 2-3in deeper.

Climbing Methods

The method plants use to climb affects the way we treat them in the garden. Even plants which are self-clinging occasionally need help by tying them in. Many climbing plants have no form of natural climbing. These usually scramble through shrubs and low branches, supporting themselves by flopping over them. These are much more in need of our help, needing to be tied to various types of support.

Some plants, such as sweet pea, have tendrils with which they grasp a support. Little attention is needed except to ensure that they have something to climb and that they climb in the right direction.

A few climbers cling on with their roots, ivy for example. This will climb walls, fences, trunks and branches. If the wall is sound or the tree is in good health, it should not cause any problems.

Training and Pruning

Fan young shoots out so that they cover a wide area rather than make a single column. Then tie them into the support if necessary. The amount of pruning required will vary with the plant, from none at all to cutting almost to the ground each year, as with some clematis. Seek advice when purchasing as to the individual climbing plant's pruning requirements.

Lathyrus odoratus 'White Supreme' (Sweet Pea)

Tying

The best way of tying the plant to its support is to form a figure-of-eight with the string, crossing it over between the plant and the support. Tie the knot at the back of the support if possible or at the side.

Wall supports

Climbing plants are useful for softening the walls of a house or for concealing an eyesore such as a garage or oil tank. In some cases it may be necessary to construct a trellis or screen. In others, the plants can be attached directly to a wall.

• The simple method of training plants on a wall is with a wooden or plastic trellis panel. It is a good idea to use blocks of wood as spacers so that there is a gap between the trellis and the wall. As an alternative, rigid plastic netting or even wire netting can be used.

• If the wall has to be painted regularly, use a trellis fixed to a frame. Attach this with hinges at the bottom so that it can be eased away from the wall without breaking the climber, allowing the wall to be painted. Use rotating blocks at the top to hold it in place.

Clematis 'Vyvyan Pennell'

• A more permanent method is to attach horizontal wires to the wall. These can be fixed with vine eyes which are hammered into the wall so that the eye is about an inch from the surface. A tensioning screw at one end will keep the wire taut.

• A less common method is to use wall ties - special nails with a lead strip attached to the head. The nail is hammered in next to the shoot and the strip wrapped around it. A simple method is to use strips of canvas or plastic doubled around the shoot and then nailed to the wall.

Freestanding supports for climbing plants

Today, there are a wide range of supports which can be used for growing climbing plants. Many of these are decorative features in their own right. Whatever method you decide on, it is essential that the support is properly anchored, making sure it is firmly in the ground. A climbing plant in full leaf will act as a sail and the wind blowing on it can exert tremendous pressure.

• Freestanding trellis panels, pergolas, arches and arbours can all be clothed with climbing plants. When calculating widths of arches etc, always allow for the thickness of the plants that will be grown up the sides.

Sweet Pea growing on a free-standing trellis obelisk

- Climbing plants can be grown through trees, shrubs and even other climbers. Clematis is one of the most popular climbers for this. Avoid using climbing plants which are too rampant, like Russian vine, which would otherwise swamp and even kill its host.

- Fences can be brightened up with climbers. They can be tied directly to a wire fence, but with a boarded fence panel you will need to attach wires. Nailing wire or plastic netting to the fence gives plenty of fixing positions.

- Temporary or more permanent supports can be made from wigwams of poles, canes or pea sticks. Annuals such as sweet pea can be grown through pea sticks and then the whole lot discarded in the winter.

Lapageria rosea (Chilean Bell Flower)

Lathyrus odoratus 'Antique Fantasy Mixed'

Favourite Climbers

Passiflora caerulea (Passion Flower)
This is one of the most exotic flowering climbing plants we can grow. The beautiful flowers are borne on fast-growing woody tendrils. It requires a warm, sunny, sheltered spot and enjoys rich, well-drained soil.

Clematis 'The President'
Rich-purple flowered clematis is the variety The President. The flowers are produced early in the season.

Lapageria rosea

Regarded as one of the most beautiful of all climbing plants, and best grown in a conservatory, it is the national flower of Chile. Lapageria produces large, waxy bells in red, pink or white. It requires lime-free soil and produces evergreen foliage. When seen in full flower, this is a sight not to be forgotten.

Clematis alpina 'Frances Rivis'

This is a free-flowering spring variety, which covers itself in beautiful mauve-blue bells with a white centre. The petals hang and, when caught by the breeze, look like dancing butterflies.

Passiflora caerulea (Passion Flower)

Clematis jackmanii 'Superba'

This is one of the most popular mid to late summer flowering clematis. It produces large velvet-purple flowers, making a spectacular show when in full bloom.

Clematis cirrhosa 'Freckles'

This is an evergreen variety which produces its red-flecked bell flowers in winter.

Clematis jackmanii 'Superba'

Clematis 'Prince Charles'

Clematis 'Prince Charles'
This produces a mass of medium-sized, sky-blue flowers. It is a very striking plant when grown in association with pale foliage or yellow flowers.

Wisteria
For sheer beauty, it is hard to beat wisteria in full flower. Though it comes in several shades, the most popular is a lilac form. Wisteria needs plenty of space to grow and is best planted in a sunny position. It is ideal at the front of a house, where it can be trained over a door and allowed to travel upwards. Wisteria should be pruned in late summer and then again in January. It is a greedy plant and benefits from an application of well-rotted manure or compost annually. It may take several years to settle in, but it is well worth waiting for.

Wisteria sinensis allowed to ramble over a bridge

Hedera (Ivy)

There are many different types of ivy and some very beautiful foliage forms. They have the great advantage of being self-clinging. One of the prettiest is the variety 'Goldheart' which produces dark green leaves with a bright golden centre. Another beauty is H. colchica dentata 'Variegata'. This has large leaves with a rich cream variegation. This particular variety benefits from some support. Ivies look well all year round, are not fussy about soil and will grow in sun or shade. They can be slow to establish and may take a little while to take off, but once they start into good growth, they will cover a wall rapidly. They can easily be controlled by cutting and pruning.

Jasminum polyanthum

A magnificent climbing plant, grown for its fabulous fragrance, is Jasminum polyanthum. This requires a sheltered sunny spot outside or the protection of a sunny conservatory or glass porch. It produces a mass of white, pink-tinted, buds which open into clusters of star-shaped flowers.

Vitis coignetiae

Commonly called the crimson glory vine, it makes a magnificent climber for the colour of its autumn foliage, which turns brilliant colours from amber to crimson. It is a large-growing climbing plant that needs plenty of space.

Hedera 'Goldheart' trained into ball shape in a container. This grows equally well if trained against a wall where it can self-cling

Hints

Sweet Pea

Soak sweet pea seed overnight before sowing. Blue varieties take longer to germinate than others so do be patient.

Wisteria

For the longest flower trusses on a wisteria (sometimes up to 3ft in length), select the variety 'Macrobotrys'.

Self-clinging climbers

Don't plant self-clinging climbers such as ivy on old crumbly bricks or mortar; they will be perfectly safe however on sound masonry or brickwork.

Actinidia

To obtain the best leaf coloration on the attractive climber Actinidia kolomikta, it must be planted against a warm wall and, even then, only in the early part of the summer and when the plant is well established will the variegation be seen at its best.

Clematis

For the best orange colour among the late-summer-flowering clematis species, choose Clematis tangutica 'Bill Mackenzie'.

Honeysuckle

Plant climbing honeysuckles in the more wild parts of the garden where they can climb over old tree stumps, fence posts or up into living trees. Their straggly, loose habit is never satisfactorily contained on a formal trellis or house wall.

'*Lathyrus odoratus* 'Matucana' – One of the finest sweet peas introduced into cultivation around 1700 by a Sicilian monk. Its scent is noticeably stronger than modern varieties

Care Calendar

January

Climbers to prune now: wisteria, ivy, ornamental vines, Boston ivy, climbing hydrangea and Virginia creeper.

February

If there is snow make sure to brush it off climbers as, if it accumulates, it can break stems.

March

Winter-flowering jasmine can be pruned this month.

April

Tie in shoots of twiners such as clematis.

May

Prune Clematis montana after it has flowered.

June

Propagate climbers such as wisteria and honeysuckle by layering.

July

Prune wisteria by cutting back all whippy growth to five or six buds from the main stem.

August

Complete summer pruning of wisteria. This will encourage the plant to produce flower buds for next year.

September

Prepare ground this month for planting new climbers.

October

Plant container grown climbers now making sure you have prepared the soil well in advance.

November

Tie in long and whippy growth to prevent them being blown and damaged by bad weather.

December

Take hardwood cuttings of deciduous climbers.

Old wooden wheelbarrow surrounded by *Clematis* 'Bee's Jubilee'

Iris germanica hybrid (Bearded Iris)

Perennials

Alstroemeria 'Red Elf' – Once established, this is a strong growing perennial

Perennials are long-lived and very versatile plants. These are the plants which will come back bigger and better every year. There is a huge choice and array to choose from – everything from old-fashioned cottage garden favourites like delphiniums, lupins and peonies to perennials which will grow in woodland conditions, for example primulas, hellebores and hostas. You will be able to find a perennial to suit most aspects and soil conditions. They are generally versatile and easy-to-grow.

A perennial is simply a plant that completes its life cycle over many years. This includes trees and shrubs. But when using the term perennial in gardening we usually mean herbaceous perennials. In other words, a plant which dies down at the end of the growing and flowering season to re-emerge the following spring to continue its life cycle.

Perennial plants will live for as long as you wish them to providing that you are prepared to divide them or take cuttings. Though there are some perennials,

Hemerocallis 'Moonlit Masquerade'

like lupins and aquilegias, which are short-lived, others such as peonies can live undisturbed for twenty years or more.

Buying Perennials

Garden centres offer a large range of perennials with new and interesting varieties becoming available all the time. Perennials are grown in plastic containers and can be planted at any time of year, subject to weather and soil conditions. Ideal planting times are spring and autumn, but providing you are willing to water perennials can also be planted throughout the summer months.

Diascia 'Ruby Field'

Growing from Seed

Many perennials can be grown very easily from seed. This is a great way of raising larger quantities of plants both quickly and inexpensively. Some perennials such as verbena, gaillardia and iceland poppies will flower in their first year if you sow the seed early enough. Many others will flower in their second year and onwards.

Cutting Back

During the autumn and into early winter it is necessary to cut back dead stems of perennials to the ground. This will clean up beds and borders and the remaining supporting stakes and canes can be removed. This is an ideal time also to remove perennial and annual weeds. Autumn is a great time to mulch the bed with well-rotted farmyard manure or garden compost.

Dead-heading

Cutting off the stems of dead flowers serves two purposes. In some cases, to encourage a plant to produce a second crop of flowers, for example with lupins, delphiniums and pyrethrums. With every kind of perennial it helps to maintain the plant's strength by preventing it from putting all of its energy into setting seed. Dead-head perennials as soon as the flowers have died, or you will be left with unattractive spikes.

Protecting

A few common perennials are not completely hardy and may succumb to frost in cold areas in winter. Examples include agapanthus, penstemon and

Papaver orientalis – should be cut back after flowering

Paeonia mlokosewitschii – with patience can be grown from seed

osteospermum. As a precaution protect such plants during winter with a layer of straw, enclosing and securing this with netting.

Soil Preparation

Once you have chosen your planting site, remove perennial weeds and destroy them. You should dig the soil well in advance of planting, allowing it time to settle. Add well-rotted farmyard manure or garden compost afterwards. Before planting it can be helpful to mark the intended positions with twigs. Use a trowel or spade depending on the size of the root or container. Set your plants in groups of three or five rather than individually and do not be tempted to plant them too closely together. By planting in groups you will achieve a greater impact.

Feeding

Early spring is an ideal time to give established perennials a general balanced feed. Sprinkle the fertiliser evenly around the plant at approximately 2oz to the square metre. This is a general rule and it is important

Anthemis tinctoria 'E. C. Buxton' – light support needed when in full flower

Lobelia 'Queen Victoria' – Requires a moist position and will need watering in dry spells

to follow the instructions given on the pack. If this is the first application to newly planted perennials, generally a little more can be given.

Watering

Perennials are best grown in continuously moist soil. This should be maintained during dry spells. One of the best ways to water perennials is to use a perforated or leaky hose. Also, mulching perennials in late spring helps to conserve moisture.

Supporting

Tall perennials, for example delphiniums, can flop easily without support. Wind can play havoc. Proprietary support systems can be bought, but three or four bamboo canes with string tied between them are a simple, reliable method. Supports should be put in place while the plants are only half grown, with the bamboo canes angled slightly outwards. These will soon be hidden.

10 Easy-to-Grow Perennials

Agapanthus

This is one of my favourite perennials. The blue flowers in mid to late summer create a magnificent show. They grow approximately 3ft in height with a 30in spread. They require full sun and can also be grown in containers.

Anemone x hybrida

Another favourite perennial and superb for adding late summer interest. They come in pink or white, growing approximately 2.5 - 4ft in height when in full flower, with a spread of approximately 18in - 2ft.

Dianthus 'Mrs. Sinkins'

Anemone x hybrida 'September Charm'

Astrantia major

Dicentra spectabilis 'Goldheart' (Bleeding Heart) —
This variety is noted for its golden foliage

Primula 'Guinevere'

Papaver orientale 'Patty's Plum'

Helleborus x hybridus 'Ashwood Garden' hybrids

Aster (Michaelmas Daisy)

There are a great number of different varieties ranging in colour from white, pink and red to blue. They range from dwarf to as tall as 5ft in height. They require a sunny position and flower from late summer into autumn.

Dicentra (Bleeding Heart)

Grows to approximately 18in to 2ft in height and has beautiful heart-shaped flowers which hang like little pendants in late spring. They grow best in sun or light shade.

Helleborus x hybridus

These grow from 18in to 2ft in height. They come in a wide range of colours — purple, white, pink, some are even spotted. They enjoy light shade and flower from late winter to mid spring.

Meconopsis betonicifolia

Paeonia tenuifolia rosea

Meconopsis betonicifolia

A beautiful perennial which requires a cool, moist position. Stunning blue poppy flowers with golden centres, growing 3-4ft in height and flowering late spring into early summer. Grows well in light shade.

Peonies

Peonies are long-lived plants which flower in early summer. They need a sunny, open spot and vary in colour from white, crimson, pink, to yellow.

Primula denticulata (Drumstick Primula)

Available in white, mauve or red. They grow to approximately 12in in height, growing well in sun or shade, and flower in mid spring.

Aquilegias (Columbine)

These grow to approximately 1 to 2ft. They flower in early summer and the spurred flowers come in many different colours and colour combinations. An old-fashioned name for this plant was 'Granny's Bonnet' because of the flower shape. It will grow well in sun or shade.

Campanula persicifolia

Beautiful bells of white or pale pink. Growing approximately 2ft height and flowering in mid summer. To flower well they need sun.

Galega officinalis

Foxgloves

To maintain a white population of foxgloves, pull out any plants with pink flowers before their blooms actually open: this will prevent any cross pollination occurring. The common species of foxgloves are short-lived. For something different, why not try some of the perennial types?

Paeonies

Move paeony plants just as growth is beginning in spring and do so with the minimum possible disturbance to the large, fleshy tubers. In this way, you will be less likely to lose a season's flowers.

Hints

New border

When planting a new mixed or shrub border, make use of annuals to fill in the gaps, until the larger plants have matured. Plant herbaceous and bedding plants in groups of three or five to achieve a more rapid and effective display.

Simple support

For the easiest, most efficient and inconspicuous method of giving support to herbaceous perennials, use L-shaped interlocking supports of plastic-covered wire or semi-circular metal hoops. Install stakes or other supports for herbaceous perennials when they are about 20-30 cm (8-12 in) tall. If you leave them until they are much taller than this you will be likely to damage their stems.

Delphiniums

In windy gardens, traditional, tall-stemmed delphiniums can be a frustrating disappointment. Instead, therefore, try such shorter growing varieties as 'Blue Tit' (dark blue) or 'Mighty Atom' (lilac).

Thin out late bloomers

In late spring, thin out the shoots on late-summer-flowering herbaceous perennials such as Michaelmas daisies to obtain a stronger, better display of flowers.

Mildew-free daisies

The best Michaelmas daisy varieties to grow if you are plagued with mildew are those derived from Aster novae-angliae, A. x frikartii and A. x thompsonii.

Lupinus 'Thundercloud' (Lupin)

Lupins

If lupins are to your liking, then the best varieties to grow are the modern 'New Hybrids', but you should be aware that in most parts of the country all lupins will be severely attacked by the very large lupin aphid.

Himalayan blue poppies

The so-called Himalayan blue poppies of the genus Meconopsis are among the most sought-after border plants, but they are not always easy to grow, one of the problems being that most are monocarpic – they die after flowering. To avoid losing a good flowering strain such as those in the M. x sheldonii crosses, remove the flowering spikes from a few of the shoots each year before they elongate. In this way, while parts of the clump may die, others will continue.

Angel's fishing rod

The wand flower or angel's fishing rod (Dierama) is a graceful plant for late summer, but many gardeners have difficulty with it as they forget that it is evergreen and its foliage must not be cut back at the end of the season.

Aquilegias

Stout-stemmed perennials that require no staking are always valuable if you are looking for a low-maintenance garden. Aquilegias are among the best of these for spring flowering.

Carnations and pinks

When staking border carnations, be sure that the support still allows the flower head to flop slightly. This is its natural habit and prevents rain from collecting in the head and spoiling it. Replace pinks and border carnations every four years with fresh stock.

Lychnis chalcedonica, a super mid summer flowering perennial

Care Calendar

January
Clear weeds from around plants.

February
Check your stocks of stakes and supports for the season ahead.

March
Lift and divide overgrown clumps.

April
Plant new plants this month, giving them time to establish while the weather is still mild and wet.

May
Sow seeds of perennials outside. This is an economical way of raising many plants.

June
Cut back oriental poppies when they have finished flowering.

July
Divide bearded irises, keeping the best rhizomes for replanting.

August
Cut back perennials that have collapsed or spread over your lawn.

September
This is an ideal time for planting new perennials which will have a chance to establish for the following year.

October
Lift and divide overgrown clumps of perennials this month.

November
Pot up lily-of-the-valley rhizomes to force them into flower early.

December
Cut down dead growth of herbaceous perennials. Weed and tidy around plants.

Geranium psilostemon growing alongside *Hosta* 'Frances Williams'

Tulips and alliums grown in a mixed border of perennials and old-fashioned roses

Bulbs

I can remember visiting the Keukenhoff, the Dutch bulb industry's showgrounds, and being overwhelmed at the spectacular display, all provided by bulbs. Everything from hyacinth and daffodils to tulips - every imaginable bulb was on display in every imaginable colour. I realised on this visit the importance and value of using bulbs to provide colour, fragrance and interest. Bulbs make up some of our most important garden plants and if used wisely can provide year-round interest in your garden.

For reward without effort, bulbs surely take the first prize. Many of them will grow in either full sun or shade and in practically any soil providing it is not waterlogged. With the minimum of attention, they will go on and on producing flowers year after year.

Bulb Types

Here I use the term bulb loosely. There are many different types, all with one thing in common – they produce an underground swollen stem, which is used as a store by the plant while dormant.

True Bulb

These are the most typical bulbs you will come across. They are oval or round in shape and their structure is the same as an onion, being made up of layers of scales.

Tuber

A tuber is a swollen stem. A potato is a typical example of a tuber. They have no standard shape. Most tubers get larger as the plant grows. Begonia and cyclamen are two well-known examples.

Lilium tigridum hybrid (True bulb)

Corm

Most, but not all, corms are rounded or flattened bulbous plants. The nutrient-holding part is a swollen stem and not a series of scales like that of a true bulb. Examples are gladiolus and crocus.

Rhizome

This is a thickened stem. It's different from the others in that it grows horizontally. It spreads and is either completely or partially buried by soil. Examples are canna and agapanthus.

Tuberous Roots

The most common example of a tuberous root is possibly the dahlia. This is a swollen root, borne in clusters from a crown. This crown develops at the base of the old stems. Examples include alstroemeria and eremurus.

Buying Bulbs

When purchasing bulbs, it is essential to buy the best quality available. Look out for large bulbs as these will provide the biggest and best flowers. Do not be tempted by bargains as these can often be undersized and inferior in quality. With bulbs, the term 'you get what you pay for' is very true. Inspect the bulbs if they are loose, making sure that they are firm and that there is no sign of damage or rot. With small bulbs, like miniature daffodils and snowdrops, it is important to plant immediately as these small bulbs are the first to dehydrate in the warmth of a garden centre.

Dahlia 'Arabian Night'

Bulbs in Containers

Autumn is the time to plant tubs, window boxes, pots and containers in general with bulbs, which will give a cheerful spring display. Hyacinth, crocus, dwarf varieties of narcissi and the shorter types of tulips are especially suitable. Fill the containers with a free-draining compost, but first check that the drainage holes in the base are unobstructed. Then fill the bottom of the container with pieces of broken polystyrene or old broken pottery to prevent the drainage holes from becoming blocked. Once the display has finished and before the foliage dies down, the bulbs can be lifted and planted elsewhere in the garden to build up their reserves for the following year. This frees up your containers to be planted with summer flowering plants.

Bulb Care

Bulb Planting

Late summer or early autumn is the best time to plant spring-flowering bulbs. Plant summer-flowering bulbs in spring. Bulbs grow best in soil that is well drained and contains a reasonable amount of organic matter. However, any manure that is dug in before planting must be completely rotted. Organic fertilisers are best.

The usual rule is to plant bulbs in holes three times deeper than their height, for example, a 6 inch hole for bulbs 2in in height. Plant with a trowel. Suggested spacings should be taken as a rough guide. Irregular planting gives a more pleasing effect than plants grown in precisely spaced rows. Just bear the average figure in mind when placing the bulbs on the

Erythronium (Dog's Tooth Violet)

ground in random order before planting. Small groups of bulbs always look better than single plants.

Clear the ground of all weeds first so that the soil will not have to be disturbed again after planting. Where bulbs and spring bedding are grown together, plant the biennials first. Leave the spaces for groups of bulbs to be planted afterwards.

Generally bulbs should be planted as soon as possible after you have purchased them. An exception to this rule is tulips, which are best planted late in the season – November is ideal. Bulbs should be planted while they are still firm and preferably without any sign of growth.

Feeding

If you are growing bulbs in containers it is most important to use a liquid feed. Once the food

Fritillaria imperialis 'Aureomarginata'

Allium 'Globemaster'

reserves of the compost have completely exhausted, you will need to use a liquid feed or even a slow-release feed to sustain the bulbs. If the quality of your soil in your garden is good and if you mulch with well-rotted compost or manure there is very little need for feeding outdoors. A light application of a general fertiliser after flowering can help restore flowering energy for the following year.

After Flowering

After flowering it is very important to allow the bulb to restore its energy so that it can multiply and flower for the following year. It is also a good idea to dead-head so that energy is not wasted on developing seedpods. Do not cut or remove the foliage, as this is the bulb's way of manufacturing nutrients to be stored within the bulb. To remove the foliage will only weaken the developing bulb.

Naturalising Bulbs

The term naturalising means planting bulbs in grass or under trees where they can be left undisturbed for many years. Crocuses and narcissi are favourites for this purpose. Snowdrops look good when planted beside a hedge or under a deciduous shrub. Although bulbs can be naturalised in a lawn, a rougher area is better as the grass will have to be left uncut until the bulb foliage dies down. This can take as long as 5-6 weeks after the flowers have finished. Aim for a natural, informal effect. To do this, scatter the bulbs at random over the area to be planted, mixing different sorts if you like, and plant them where they fall. Avoid the temptation to even out the spacings. For planting, there are special bulb planters that taken out a neat core of soil. Alternatively, lift flaps of turf. Loosen the soil beneath with a hand fork and then replace the turf after planting.

Galanthus (Snowdrop)

Cyclamen coum
Height: 3in; Spacing: 5in

Pink or white flowers in winter. Likes shade. Plant in early autumn.

Colchicum autumnale (Autumn crocus)
Height: 6-9in; Spacing: 9in

Flowers are pink and crocus-like in autumn. Will grow in sun or shade. Plant in summer.

Crocuses
Height: 4-5in; Spacing: 4-5in

There are numerous varieties. Some are autumn flowering and some are spring flowering. They come in white, yellow, blue or purple. Like a sunny position and best planted in late summer to early autumn.

Fritillaria meleagris (Snake's Head Fritillary)
Height: 12in; Spacing: 6in

Flowers come in purple or white and are chequered. They have a bell-like shape and flower in spring. Will grow in sun or shade. Plant in autumn.

Hyacinthus
Height: 9in; Spacing: 6in

Fragrant. Pink, blue white or yellow flowers in spring. Sun or light shade. Plant in autumn.

Crocosmia masoniorum 'Rowallane Yellow'

Hyacinth hybrid – noted for its magnificent fragrance

Muscari armenianicum (Grape hyacinth)

Height: 8in; Spacing: 3-4in

Blue or white spikes in spring. They need a sunny position. Plant in early autumn.

Tulipa

Height: 8-30in; Spacing: 4-8in

Come in a great range of colours, flower shapes and sizes in spring. Need sun and shelter. Plant in late autumn.

Anemone coronaria

Height: 9in; Spacing: 5in

Come in single or double flowered in a range of bright colours in spring or autumn depending on the time of planting. Will grow in sun or shade. Plant in autumn or spring.

Gladiolus (Sword Lily)

Height: 18in – 4ft; Spacing: 4-6in

There are many hybrid types, including miniatures. Flower in summer. Plant in spring.

Narcissus (Daffodil)

Height: 3in – 2 ft; Spacing: 2in – 8in

There is a remarkable range of species and varieties available with gold, red, apricot and white being the dominant colours in spring. They grow well in sun or light shade and are best planted in early autumn.

Narcissus 'Fairy Gold'

Iris reticulata 'Springtime'

Hints

Daffodils

Don't knot the foliage of daffodils: it impairs their functioning – and looks terrible. For the earliest daffodil flowers, two of the most reliable types are the tiny hoop-petticoat Narcissus bulbocodium or the more conventionally bloomed 'February Gold'.

Cyclamen for winter

To take over when the Cyclamen hederifolium finishes flowering in autumn, plant the less frequently seen winter- and spring-blooming C. coum.

Nerines

Plant nerine bulbs just below the surface – rather like shallots, with the tops poking through.

Propagating snowdrops

Transplant and divide snowdrops and aconites after the flowers have faded but while they are still in full leaf – they establish much better this way than as dry bulbs.

Crown imperials

Plant crown imperial bulbs on their sides to prevent water collecting round the crown and causing decay.

Gladioli

When lifting gladioli, carefully pull away the baby cormlets, store them separately and the pot them up in the spring. Keep them in pots for a couple of years by which time, with liquid feeding, they

Fritillaria imperialis 'Aurea' (Crown Imperial)

should be large enough to plant out in the garden. Do not plant all of your anemone and gladiolus corms at the same time: plant a few at a time over a period of a few weeks to give a succession of blooms. Allow a hundred days between planting gladiolus corms and the time you want the flowers. If the tall, large-flowered gladioli are not entirely to your taste, try the smaller and more delicately bloomed butterfly varieties.

Hyacinths

To be certain of having a uniform bowl of hyacinths, buy slightly more bulbs than you actually require and raise each separately in a 10cm (4in) pot. Then choose the most uniform group and arrange them, still in their pots, in the bowl and pack them round with bulb fibre. After indoor hyacinths have finished flowering, cut off the old flower spike, give the plants liquid fertiliser and then, when the foliage dies down, lift and store the bulbs until the autumn when they can be planted in the garden. Use sprigs of winter flowering shrubs such as forsythia to give support to the blooms of hyacinths growing in bowls – but take care to avoid unpleasant colour clashes.

Red and purple parrot tulips with Globemaster alliums

Hyacinthus orientalis 'Woodstock'

Tulips

After lifting tulip or other bulbs for storage, allow them to dry briefly – but never in direct sun, which can cause serious damage. After tulips have finished flowering, lift the plants carefully and replant them temporarily in an inconspicuous part of the garden until the foliage has died down. It yellows most unattractively and can spoil the appearance of an ornamental border.

Lilium regale growing in large containers with Lutyens-style garden bench

Formal lawn surrounded with low box hedge

Lawns

You can compare a lawn to a carpet in a living-room. It helps to pull everything together and somehow if your lawn looks well then so does your garden. To make a new lawn takes a little bit of time, but it is time which is well worth spending as the results of your efforts will give you a beautiful lawn which you will enjoy for a very long time. There are many reasons for starting a new lawn. You may have just moved into a new house and be faced with a pile of builder's debris, you may have inherited a lawn which is beyond repair, or you may be redesigning your garden and creating a re-shaped lawn.

Soil Preparation

The first step with any new lawn is preparing the soil, making sure it is in good condition and, most importantly, making sure it is level. If you have moved into a new house where builders have left rubbish behind or, in some cases, the builder may have spread topsoil which is only covering broken bricks and bits and pieces from the building process, it may be necessary in these cases to actually bring in extra, good quality topsoil. This might sound like a lot of hard work, but I guarantee you that you will only need to do it once and it will make all the difference in the years to come. Do not skimp. By spending a little money at this stage you will save having to dig up and replace lawn and plants at a later stage.

Also at this point, it is a good idea to check that you are happy with the drainage of your garden. A waterlogged lawn will not thrive and it may mean starting from scratch at a later date. If drainage is needed, it's a good idea to consult an expert as each site can vary and you do not want to compound the problem.

Growing from Seed

The best time to sow seed is just as the soil warms up in April or again in late August into September while the soil is still warm but the rainfall begins to increase. Sowing seed is inexpensive and there is a wide range of different seed mixes to choose from. Your first consideration is to ascertain what kind of wear and tear the lawn is going to get. You can choose seed from three basic categories: fine, medium and hardwearing. The hardwearing contains more rye grass. This is a tougher type of grass, which will tolerate children playing and a limited amount of wear and tear from pets like dogs. The medium and finer grade seeds will require a little more maintenance and will be less tolerant of overuse.

You will need to give a new lawn grown from seed at least six months to establish before it can be exposed to any types of wear and tear.

Preparing the Soil

If you are renovating and working with an old lawn, you will need to spray the existing lawn with weedkiller and let it die. Then dig and break up the soil, removing stones as you go. If the soil is very poor this is the stage when you will need to add some organic matter or even fresh topsoil. Then you will need to rake and firm the soil. It is worthwhile to take some extra time to level this soil as it is much easier to correct bumps and hollows at this stage.

Sowing the Seed

Before sowing the seed it is a good idea to water the ground and let weed seeds germinate. These can be sprayed with a weedkiller. This will help to clean the surface if there is a lot of weed seed in the soil and gives the new grass an easier time to establish. Now you are ready to sprinkle your seed. When working your way across the site, use an old piece of board or a plank to help distribute your weight so that you are not making hollows in the even soil. Two boards

will be adequate, working your way backwards from the top of the lawn.

The Roll-Out Lawn

Nowadays a roll-out lawn, known as turfing, is much more commonly available. This can be laid, weather permitting, most of the year, though spring and autumn are the optimum time for this job. You can even walk on your new lawn after a few weeks and it will tolerate wear and tear in just a few months. The key is to buy good quality, weed-free turf and it must be laid as soon as it is delivered. Therefore, it is important to have your soil preparation carried out in advance and also to keep a close eye on weather conditions so you are able to carry out the job immediately.

1. Look at a sample before you buy. It is important to look for uniformity in thickness. Make sure that there are no weeds and also check that you are happy with the quality of soil that comes with the turf. It is important also to look at the root system, making sure it holds and binds the turf strongly together.

2. Preparing the soil. Do this as you would for sowing grass seed. You can rake in some fertiliser and make sure that the area is level.

3. Lay the first rows of turves and gently tamp them down. A board laid on the new grass will help you avoid compacting the loose soil. It helps to

distribute the weight of your body and it will also firm in the new turves.

4. Lay the second row. It is important to start with a half-turf, as this will stagger the joints like that of bricks.

5. Once the turves are laid, brush in some good compost or fine topsoil into the cracks. This will help to knit the turves together and also will help to prevent edges drying out and shrinkage.

6. Trim and shape the edges and water your new lawn thoroughly. From this stage watering will be the key to success. You must never let the turves dry out or they will shrink and the grass at the edge will die. Do not depend on rain. It will be necessary to use a hose and sprinkler until the turves knit together.

7. Make the first mowing after a few weeks. It is important that the blades are at their highest setting. It is also a good idea to make sure that the blades are at their sharpest so that they will cut cleanly without tugging at the turves.

Moss

One of the most common questions I am asked about lawns is how to deal with moss. Moss is often at its worst when the soil is damp or if the soil is very acidic or compacted. It also can be a problem in shady areas where grass doesn't grow well and the

soil remains damp. You can use a proprietary moss killer to deal with existing moss. It is essential to rake this out when it turns black, but you will also need to work out why the moss is a problem in the first place.

Raking
Moss thrives in old, choked lawns. Scarifying every autumn and gently raking in spring helps.

Top-dressing
If your soil is poor, acidic, or even sandy, you can reduce moss by top-dressing after scarifying and then aerate in the autumn.

Mowing
Regular mowing at the correct height will thicken grass and help to reduce moss.

Feeding
If your lawn is well fed and growing strongly, there should be no room for moss.

Lawnmowers

There are basically two types of lawnmower: the cylinder mower would be my first choice. This acts like a scissors, cutting the grass between the rotating blades and the static base blade. If the cylinder mower has a roller, it will help to create a beautiful classic striped pattern after cutting. To maintain a cylinder mower blades will require frequent adjustment. They can also be more expensive, but the result is a superior cut. The other type of lawnmower is a rotary mower. The blades swirl, creating a slashing action. If the blades are kept sharp, it will cut the grass well. These mowers are usually easier to maintain and also easier to clean. The major problem I find with rotary mowers is that gardeners do not keep the blades sharp and this can cause "split-ends" on the grass which can create a light browning effect on your lawn. If you are using an electric mower, it is a good idea to purchase a residual circuit power breaker. This is a safety device which can help prevent a serious accident.

Mowing

It is important to mow your lawn on a regular basis. Do this whether you think your lawn needs mowing or not. By mowing your lawn on a regular basis, you help to keep it healthy. Little and often is the trick. This will help to thicken the grass, not allowing room for weeds to invade. Always remove grass clippings and cut your grass to a height of 20-30mm. Only the finest, well-maintained lawns should be cut shorter. No lawn should be cut under a height of 12mm.

Killing Weeds

Most weedkillers are applied as granules. The best way to apply these is with a lawn spreader. This is a very handy tool as it spreads at the correct rate, guaranteeing you an economical use of your weedkiller. Granulated weedkillers are usually a combination of fertiliser and weedkiller and are

usually as fast-working as a liquid. The best time to use these is between April and early July. You can keep weeds down by looking after your lawn and feeding it properly. A starved lawn grows more slowly, giving weeds a chance to establish and take hold. Only use a lawn weedkiller if you are prepared to follow the instructions. These lawn weedkillers will not harm the grass, whereas a general weedkiller will kill all plants. Lawn weedkillers work best when the weeds are growing fast. This is when the weather is warm and the soil is moist. If you have a bad infestation it is a good idea to feed lawn and weeds before applying a weedkiller as the extra stimulation in growth that comes from the feed will assist the lawn weedkiller in its task.

10 Tips for the Perfect Lawn

- Make sure you prepare the seedbed well.

- Sow your lawn using the highest quality blend of seed available, repairing patches if they appear.

- Mow your lawn regularly and avoid cutting too low.

- Water your lawn frequently in dry conditions.

- Feed with a nitrogen-rich fertiliser in spring or early summer and a balanced fertiliser in the early autumn.

- Rake out old grass during spring and autumn.

- Scatter worm casts with a brush before mowing and remove all the clippings.

- On heavy soil, aerate your lawn in spring and again in summer.

- Control any weeds and moss. Don't wait until the lawn is infested.

- Trim the edges.

Formal Italian garden with lawn

Wear and tear

To minimise grass wear and tear at the places where you step on to the lawn, peg down heavy duty plastic netting. As the grass grows, the net will disappear into the turf but still provide support in the soil to prevent damage.

Cylinder is best

For the best possible finish on a fine lawn, use a cylinder rather than a rotary mower.

Weedkiller on lawns

Don't use weedkiller on the spring lawn until the weather is warm and the soil moist.

Hints

Improved drainage

To improve the drainage on your lawn, hire (they are too costly to justify buying) a powered hollow-tine lawn spiker which removes plugs of soil.

Good old-fashioned weeding

For a small lawn, with few deep-rooted weeds, don't bother with chemical controls but use a V-shaped daisy grubber instead – an old-fashioned tool, but one that is still extremely useful.

Keep off frozen grass

Don't walk on the lawn when the grass is frozen: you will break the grass blades and leave brown marks that will persist until the spring.

Grasses hate shade

Don't try to establish grasses beneath the shade of large trees. They will never grow there satisfactorily and you will constantly be plagued with bare patches, weeds and moss.

Edge repairs

To repair a broken edge of a lawn, cut a square of turf round the broken portion, turn it so that the broken part faces inwards and re-lay it. You will then have a firm edge while the damaged part may be packed with compost and seeded.

Dressing a new lawn

Use autumn lawn fertiliser as a base dressing when sowing or laying a new lawn.

Lawn with diagonal stripe created by mowing with a cylinder lawn mower

Trug with organically grown vegetables

Vegetables

Today, there is great interest in what we eat. We are more aware of organic vegetables than ever before. There are concerns about the genetic modification of the vegetables we eat and many worry about the commercial sprays that are applied to crops. Also, the regulation of food crops means that some of the old-fashioned varieties, which were grown for

Sea kale with sea kale forcers

flavour rather than large yield, are no longer available in supermarkets or fruit and vegetables shops. So the opportunity to grow your own home-grown vegetables is now more attractive than ever before. You do not need a large garden. An interesting range can be grown even in the smallest of spaces.

By growing your own vegetables you are able to grow them organically and you can harvest them without the fear of contamination with potentially dangerous chemicals. Another great advantage is that you can grow varieties which have stood the test of time and are noted for exceptional flavour. It is also possible to grow vegetables which may be scarce or generally unobtainable.

There is nothing that can compare to growing, harvesting and cooking your own vegetables. It's one of the most satisfying and rewarding aspects of gardening.

Onions being allowed to dry for storage

Crop Rotation

Never grow vegetables in the same patch year after year. Over the centuries vegetables have been grown in a very particular rotation system, simply known as crop rotation. This has several advantages. It helps to sustain the soil, preventing it from becoming exhausted quickly. It also prevents a build up of pests and diseases and helps to keep a balance of soil nutrients.

To rotate crops, you will need to set up a three-year plan. Divide your vegetable plot into three equal areas. You can create a fourth area where you grow permanent vegetables such as asparagus. This could be a simple strip of land at the end of the plot.

Wigwam with runner beans

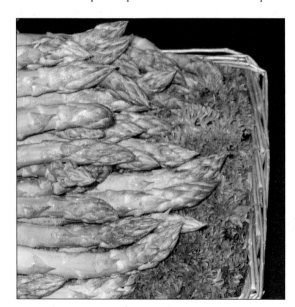
Asparagus tips

It can also be used for plants like rhubarb. You leave this area outside of your three-year rotation plan.

The first divided area in your plot becomes year one, the second year two and the third year three. In the first section set out an area for growing root vegetables such as parsnip, carrots, potatoes, beetroot, etc. In the centre section, lay out an area for brassicas such as cabbage, cauliflower, broccoli, Brussels sprouts, turnips swedes and kale. In the last section grow other vegetables. For example beans, celery, leeks, lettuce, peas, onions, sweet corn etc. The following year the root crops will move to the centre position, following the brassicas. Then the brassicas move on to where the other crops were. So each year, each crop moves on one section.

The soil in each section will need very particular attention each year. For your root crops do not add manure and do not lime. Add a general fertiliser 2-3 weeks before sowing or planting. In your brassica section the soil will require well-rotted manure or garden compost. Lime the soil in this area only if you are sure it is not already alkaline. As before, rake in a general fertiliser 2-3

Courgette 'Venus F1 Hybrid'

weeks before planting. For your other crops dig in a good quantity of well-rotted manure or garden compost. Lime is only required if the soil is acidic and again rake in a general fertiliser 2-3 weeks before sowing or planting.

An example of how this system works to keep fertility is peas are always followed by brassicas. The reason for this is that brassicas are generally leafy crops which require a lot of nitrogen to keep them healthy. The peas which they follow are nitrogen fixing. The root system of pea plants traps nitrogen adding it to the soil,

Vegetable crops growing within a walled garden

Salad crops in a raised bed system with bamboo wigwam

catch cropping. This is where you will sow a quick-maturing crop such as French beans, lettuce, radishes, spring onions, turnips or beetroot. These crops can be harvested in time before autumn digging and your rotation moves on.

Successional Sowing

There are many vegetable crops that do not store well, for example, lettuce. To avoid a glut of them it is necessary to sow short rows every few weeks. This will guarantee you a succession to harvest, prolonging the use of the crop without creating a glut.

The Raised Bed System

In a small garden it can be very handy to use the raised bed system. Create separate plots, approximately 5ft square. Surround these with some pre-treated timber boards. This prevents soil toppling onto paths and allows you to cultivate within, raising the soil above ground level. This will allow you to double dig and to incorporate heavy dressings of manure or garden compost. Your vegetables can be sown in blocks on the bed. This means that all of your vegetables are at the same distance from each other. The spacings are quite close so that the leaves of the adjacent plants touch as the plants come to maturity. All of your cultivation is carried out from the paths between the beds. Weeds are completely suppressed and the yield is far greater than that obtained by growing your vegetables using the row system.

so the brassicas have an extra supply of nitrogen once the roots of the peas have been left behind. This helps to sustain good fertility.

Catch Cropping

While maintaining your vegetables in a crop rotation, there will be periods when important crops have finished and bare patches become exposed. Take advantage of these bare patches by

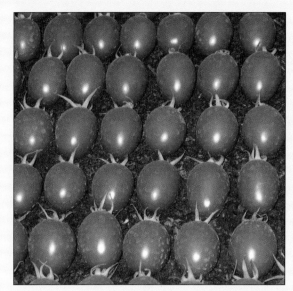

Plum tomatoes

Hints

Catch crops

To make the best use of your kitchen garden space, grow fast-growing radishes or lettuces as catch crops – sow them where the rows of larger and more slowly maturing crops have been lifted, or in the gaps between rows of peas.

Deep bed

The best labour-saving way of growing vegetables is on a deep bed. Double dig a bed about 1.2m (4ft) wide and as long as space permits and incorporate large volumes of organic matter.

Thereafter, avoid walking on the bed when planting, feeding, cultivating or harvesting (use a brick and plank 'bridge' if it helps). In this way, soil compaction will be minimised and digging should only be necessary every five years or so.

Equal spacing

The most efficient way of growing most types of vegetable is to space them equidistantly, rather than in rows where there will be small gaps between the plants but wide spaces between the rows.

Flower harvest

Flowers that are intended essentially for cutting are best grown in the kitchen garden where their removal won't affect the rest of a display.

Asparagus

Grow asparagus plants in flat beds at a spacing between plants of 30cm (1ft) each way: not on ridges as traditionally suggested, unless the soil is very badly drained. Don't plant an asparagus bed until you are sure that the soil has been well cleared of perennial weeds, especially scutch. They will be very difficult to eradicate later. Don't cut asparagus spears after early June or you will weaken the plants, but do give them liquid fertiliser throughout the summer.

French beans

Pick French beans before the seeds swell sufficiently to cause bulges in the pods. For one of the finest flavoured French bean varieties, choose 'The Prince'.

Cabbage

To avoid the common problem of bolting in Chinese cabbage, choose fast-growing varieties and delay sowing until after midsummer.

After harvesting cabbages, leave the stump in the ground and cut a cross in the top. This will encourage tasty green shoots to form, giving you more return for your labours.

Leeks

When planting leeks, trim the root and leaf tips before dropping each plant into a 15cm (6in) deep hole, then fill the hole with water.

Rhubarb

If flower spikes arise on rhubarb plants, pull them away promptly or they will weaken the plants. Never pull more than a third of the stems from one rhubarb plant at a time as this will seriously weaken it.

Force a clump of rhubarb by placing an old bucket or similar vessel with a hole in the bottom over it – but don't force the same clump again for two years.

Supports for growing bags

To support tomato plants in a growing bag, insert a vertical cane in the soil behind the bag (or peg one to the wall) and use a small diagonal cane from the hole in the bag to train the plant's stem up to the vertical.

Best tomato variety

Easily the best flavoured tomato variety for greenhouse or outdoors is the small-fruited, heavy-cropping 'Gardeners' Delight' – and don't believe anyone who tells you otherwise.

Feeding tomatoes

Once the first fruit truss has set, feed greenhouse tomatoes twice a week and outdoor tomatoes once a week. When using liquid tomato feed it's important to follow the instructions and avoid making the feed at too strong a concentration. Little and often is much better for the plant.

Basket of potatoes

Scarlet runner beans can make an ornamental display. Here they are grown in a large container

Tender perennials with summer-flowering bedding in ornamental terracotta pots

Container Gardening

Hanging Baskets

Hanging baskets are incredibly versatile and, providing that they are watered and not allowed to dry out, they can provide a colourful display and can brighten up areas close to the house.

I always recommend, if you are making up a hanging basket, to buy the largest size basket as these are less likely to dry out and they provide enough compost to sustain a large and full display. The traditional hanging basket has a thick lining of moss. This helps to conserve moisture, supports the compost and gives a natural green look. There is a wide range of ready-made liners available. These are practical and convenient but they lack the charm of the old-fashioned green moss.

1. Line the basket up to about $1/3$ of the way up the sides with a good layer of moss. Then fill with compost to the top of the moss lining and firm in gently.

2. Arrange a row of plants gently teasing the foliage through the holes in the basket from the inside out. This helps to avoid having to crush the roots of the plants.

3. When the first row of plants are in place, add more moss to line the basket to $2/3$ of the way up. Then add compost to the same level, firming gently around the plants.

Lavendula stoechas (French Lavender) growing in full sunshine in a large ornamental container

4. Arrange the second row of plants in the same way as the first, placing them in the spaces between the first plants. Line to the top with moss and then fill with compost.

5. Plant the rest of the plants in the top of the basket, arranging the outer ones at a slight angle to encourage them to tumble over the side of the basket. Water thoroughly.

It is a good idea to stand the basket on a large flowerpot. This helps to keep the basket firm, preventing it from rocking while you are planting it.

When filling a hanging basket for a summer display, it is a good idea to line the moss with some plastic before adding the compost. This helps to prevent the compost drying quickly. You can also add a plastic saucer to the bottom of the basket before adding the compost. This will act as a

Ivy-leafed geraniums in hanging baskets

reservoir. You can also add a water retentive gel which comes in crystal form. This can be mixed through the compost and will help to prevent the compost going dry in summer.

If you find your basket does become too dry, it is important to lift the basket down from its bracket and to stand it in a basin of water for about a half an hour until it becomes fully re-hydrated.

It is possible to create a winter display using winter-flowering bedding plants, small bulbs, and winter-flowering heathers, combined with variegated trailing ivy to create a splash of colour through the winter months.

Baskets can be used to

- Add height to a flower display and allow you to grow bedding plants in high up places.
- Brighten up plain walls and fences adding a splash of colour.
- Hang from branches of a tree to add interest.
- Decorate a porch or entranceway to offer a cheerful welcome to visitors.
- Add a formal feel to the front of a house by adding several matching baskets.

Flower pots, containers and tubs have become ever-popular now that we are using patios, terraces and decking areas as extensions of our homes. An area of grey paving can be transformed by containers of flowers. These will bring colour and scent right up close where you are spending much of your leisure time. Containers can play their part in every area of the garden. They are portable and they can be used for everything from concealing a manhole to even covering a compost bin.

Container gardening allows you great flexibility and if you are planting containers with bedding plants and bulbs it is possible to change the display and colour schemes on a seasonal basis. The range and choice of containers available is extensive and

Val Dillon's blue hydrangea grown in lime-free soil in a large container.
Pots underneath planted with *Hosta* 'Halcyon'

drainage. It is also a good idea to raise a container off the ground, standing it on ornamental feet. With larger containers red bricks can be used. Fill the container with compost and always leave a little space at the top to create a reservoir while watering. Water your container on a regular basis and never depend on rain. It is okay to allow your compost to partially dry between watering, but never let the compost completely dry out. Watering on a daily basis may be required during summer. It will also be necessary with established plants to liquid feed on a regular basis. Use the rule 'little and often'. This will help to sustain plants, keeping them looking bright and healthy.

you can choose from wooden tubs to terracotta pots to plastic window boxes. The materials that containers are available in are constantly being added to. Stainless steel has become fashionable to create a contemporary look. Remember when choosing a container that it must complement its surroundings if it is to work successfully.

Check that the container has adequate drainage holes in its base. It is always a good idea to spread a layer of broken pieces of polystyrene or some broken pots at the base of the container to create extra

Always use a fresh potting compost for filling containers. If you wish to grow camellias, rhododendrons or azaleas use large containers and make sure to fill them with lime-free potting compost, often called ericaceous compost, as this is ideally suited to their needs. With other plants, for example bedding, small shrubs and patio roses, it is a good idea to use a soil-based compost like John Innes. This comes in different grades. Use No. 2 or 3. The soil content of this compost makes it less likely to dry out than peat-based compost.

Hints

Bunches of cut tulips displayed in French glazed terracotta pot

Bigger is better

As a rule of thumb, you will find that a pot or other outdoor plant container holding less compost than a conventional plant pot 20cm (8in) in diameter will require watering with frustrating frequency in summer.

Mind your floor

If you live in an apartment block, check the weight restrictions on your floor before introducing large plant containers – remember than 1 cubic metre (yard) of compost weights 1 tonne (2000lbs).

Clay is better

Clay pots are almost always more effective than plastic ones: they permit a better soil-water-air relationship and are much less likely to lead to waterlogging.

Quick-change window box

For window boxes, make a wooden container to fit on the window sill, line it with plastic sheet and make a few drainage holes inside, then fill it with pots of plants rather than planting directly into the box. In this way, it will be easy to change the planting arrangements as different types of plant come into flower during the course of the season.

Half barrels

Wooden half-barrels are among the cheapest of the really large types of plant container. To lengthen their lives, line them with plastic sheets so that the compost does not come into direct contact with the wood – but do remember to make drainage holes in the bottom of both the plastic and the barrel.

Moving heavy containers

When using large plant containers such as wooden half-barrels, try to position them in their intended final sites before filling them. If they do have to be moved when full, lengths of old scaffolding pipes are among the few things that are strong yet manageable enough to use as rollers.

Go for groups

Group together containers of varying sizes for maximum effect: they almost always look better than odd ones. But try to keep the types (terracotta, wood, and so forth) consistent within each group.

Don't crack your pots

When stacking terracotta pots, especially large ones, place a couple of sheets of newspaper between them. This will prevent the pots from jamming together and possibly being cracked.

Fun container planting. Here faces are brought to life with ornamental grass in foreground and a Juniper at back

Simple water garden made from a barrel making a very effective focal point in the corner of a garden

Water Gardens

A pool will bring a different dimension to your garden. It can provide a new source of interest and opens up an opportunity to grow a whole new range of plants. It also attracts wildlife and most importantly a pool can add a special focal point to your garden. I also find that water has a tranquil quality and can have a soothing and relaxing effect in the garden.

You do not need to have a stream or a natural supply of water to have a garden pool. If you like the idea of a fountain or a cascade this can be supplied by using a small pump which will simply recirculate the existing pool water. A garden pool can be formal or informal in its appearance. It can be as large or as small as you wish. It is most important to make it deep enough to avoid drastic temperature fluctuations.

Constructing a pool is within the capabilities of any gardener. The soil removed when you dig a pool can be used to build a rock garden alongside, but remember only topsoil should be used for this. Any subsoil should be dumped elsewhere. A flexible butyl rubber liner will provide the most satisfactory way of constructing a pool of almost any shape.

The position of the pool is of vital importance. It must be exposed to the sun for most of the day. Avoid placing it where autumn leaves fall in great numbers. Avoid natural hollows where water pressure from the soil beneath the pool may disturb the liner. As well as being in an open position and away from trees, a pool must be on level ground. It is a good idea to check this with a spirit level when deciding on the site. If the ground is not level, part of the pool liner will remain visible.

The minimum satisfactory depth for a pool is 15-18in. The surface area is not critical, but the smaller the pool the more difficult management can become. A pool of 5ft x 4ft is feasible, but the water in one twice the size will maintain a more even temperature, causing fewer problems. The shape of your pool is not very important as long as you keep it simple. Underneath the water the sides of the pool should drop at quite a steep angle. If possible, leave a few edges to form shelves approximately 9in below the water level. These shelves can be used to grow marginal plants. Allow 8-9in in width to support these plants.

Fountain adding drama, life and sound to a garden

There are a number of ways of constructing a garden pool. Concrete, the traditional material, may at first seem to be the most robust, but it does have disadvantages. Settlement or frost may result in hair cracks in the concrete. These in turn will lead to leaks. Also, making a concrete pool is very hard work. Ready-made fibreglass pools are very easy to install. First, dig a hole slightly larger than the pool. Then place the pool in position and fill the space around the outside with soil. Unfortunately, most of these pools are too small to give constantly good results. Pool liners made of butyl rubber provide the most satisfactory means of construction. PVC, especially the reinforced grades, is reasonably satisfactory although it does not last as long. Polythene will only last for a couple of years

Constructing a Pool with a Flexible Liner

Before ordering the liner, mark out the proposed shape of the pool to ensure that it will be in proportion to its surroundings. Use pegs and string to mark out a rectangular shape, but a hose pipe is better for showing a curved outline. Experiment if necessary with a variety of shapes and sizes until you are satisfied. A kidney-shaped pool looks attractive and it is certainly best to avoid fussy outlines.

Now take the measurements to use as a basis for ordering the liner. The length of the liner should be that of the pool plus twice the pool's maximum depth. The width of the liner should be that of the pool again, plus twice the pool's maximum depth. The same rule applies even if you have chosen an irregular outline. Be sure to base it on the maximum length and the maximum width.

1. Dig the hole, leaving shelves around part or all of the sides. Strip off a 2in layer of soil from the edges if you intend to lay paving stones to cover the edge of the liner. Remove any protruding stones and cover the bottom surface of the pool with damp sand to provide a smooth bed for the liner.

2. Lay the liner evenly over the hole, with its centre just touching the base of the pool. Do not press it

into shape. Place bricks or fairly heavy stones around the edge of the liner to hold it in place while it is filled with water. Make sure that these weights to not hang over the pool's edge.

3. Position the end of the hose over the pool and turn on the water. The weight of the water will stretch the liner, press it into shape and smooth out any wrinkles. Some of the bricks or stones can be lifted as the pool fills, but leave sufficient to keep the liner taught while you are still filling the pool.

4. When the pool is full remove the remaining bricks and trim the edge of the liner to shape, leaving a flap around the edge. This should be covered with paving stones bedded on mortar and laid to project an inch or two over the edge. Alternatively, if you wish, the lawn can extend up to the water's edge.

Iris encata – a good marginal water plant

Rock garden water cascade

Hints

Toddler hazard

Don't have a pool in a garden with very young children: a toddler can drown in a few centimetres of water. A wall fountain can bring the sound of water and be far enough out of reach to keep danger at bay.

How many fish?

When calculating the number of fish to stock your pool, reckon that you will need approximately 1cm (1/2in) of fish (excluding fins) for every 8 litres (2 gallons) of water.

Trouble-free fountain

The easiest and safest way to arrange a fountain in your garden pool is by using one of the low-voltage models — these operate through a transformer plugged into the nearest mains supply, needing only a low-voltage wire running to the pool itself.

Icy shock

Don't smash the ice of a garden pool: the shock waves could injure the fish. It is far easier to melt a hole in the ice. Half-fill a small saucepan with

A fun water feature where the water recycles

boiling water and use the base of the saucepan to gently melt a patch.

Keep fertilisers out

Never use manure, other organic matter or fertiliser (other than that specially sold for the purpose) in a garden pool. If you have pots of plants close to the edge of a pool, move then away from the edge when applying liquid fertiliser – if it runs into the water, it may harm your fish and also encourage prolific growth of algae.

Oxygenators

Don't grow Canadian pondweed as an oxygenator in your garden pool, or you risk acquiring blanket weed which seems to favour growing over this plant. Ceratophyllum and Myriophyllum are much better oxygenators.

Herons

There is no absolutely certain way to keep herons away from a garden pool. I have never found artificial birds to be at all effective and netting is most unsightly. A single strand of wire positioned around the pool edge at a height of about 15cm (6in) is as reliable a deterrent as anything. Another option is to place netting an inch or so below water level, where it won't be as noticeable.

A quiet and restful corner where a formal pool is surrounded with greenery taking full advantage of foliage texture and shape

Fish in water

Don't forget to feed the fish in your pool during mild periods in the winter when they become active.

Water-lilies

Be especially careful when choosing water-lilies to select a variety suited to the depth and area of your pool – some are extremely vigorous. Cut off the dead heads of water-lily flowers before they sink out of sight. They are large, fleshy objects and when they decay, they add significantly to the fouling of pool water.

Plant shelving

Construct a garden pool with ledges at various levels within it in order to be able to grow plants suited to different water depths.

A selection of indoor plants displaying different coloured foliage. In the centre is
the brightly variegated *Deaffembachia* (Dumb Cane)

House Plants

Some of my earliest gardening adventures were growing house plants. As a young man I learnt many gardening techniques by growing house plants. I discovered how to water correctly and how to care for plants in containers. Even if you don't have a garden, house plants offer you the opportunity to grow plants, whether they be cacti and succulents on a sunny windowsill or the most exotic of orchids – the choice is vast. Without spending a small fortune you can have fun growing some really interesting plants.

Cyrtanthus elatus (Scarborough Lily)

Choosing an Indoor Plant

Nowadays, there are thousands of different types of house plant available. The range changes with the seasons. So choosing the correct indoor plant for you is all-important. Before making your choice, it is important to decide on what you expect from your new indoor plant. There are four main groups: foliage house plants, grown for their attractive foliage; flowering house plants, grown for the colourful display they provide; flowering pot plants, which are also grown for the colour they give but are generally treated as short term or seasonal buys (for example, the Poinsettia at Christmas); and then there are cacti and succulents, which require different growing conditions.

It is important to have a spot in your home in mind and to work out the exact environmental conditions this spot will provide for your plant. With this position in mind, it will be easier to select a plant to suit and to grow well there.

Buying an Indoor Plant

As with the purchasing of all plants, I stress how important it is to buy from a reliable source. If a nursery or garden centre has a reputation for specialising in indoor plants, you are certain of getting the very best quality and advice. If in doubt, always ask for advice on whether or not the plant will suit your home.

Taking your Plants Home

When purchasing an indoor plant, remember that these plants have been grown in a greenhouse under perfect conditions. The right amount of light, warmth, humidity, etc. – so it is important when taking the plant home that you do not expose it, especially in winter, to chilling cold which could severely damage a plant that was accustomed to warm conditions. A plant can die if it is exposed to a severe shock. Make sure the plant is well wrapped and does not sit in your car for any great length of time. Bring it immediately to your home and position it in the best spot suited to it.

Plant Care

Watering

Nine out of ten indoor plants that die do so as the result of overwatering. If you master the watering of indoor plants it's true to say that you are generally mastering their care. The secret in this area is to allow your indoor plants to slightly dry between watering. It is very important when watering to avoid extremes as the majority of indoor plants dislike drying out completely or being over watered to the point of being soaking wet. The root system of an indoor plant breathes, taking carbon dioxide and oxygen in the same way as the foliage does. Too much water deprives the root system of this and causes smothering, which results in death and decay. In winter, watering should be reduced as most house plants will not be actively growing. When watering

Plumbago caprensis – This beautiful sky-blue flower makes an ideal climbing conservatory plant

in winter, it is also a good idea to use tepid water, avoiding a chill from cold water poured straight from the tap. There are always exceptions to the rule and occasionally you will find indoor plants which enjoy being stood in a little water, for example, indoor azaleas.

A plant that has been allowed to go too dry, if caught in time, should be stood in water for about 10-15 minutes and then allowed to drain. A plant which has been over-watered and caught before any damage occurs should gently be removed from its pot and stood to allow excessive moisture to evaporate from the exposed compost before being placed back into the pot again. Remember the rule, do not expose your indoor plants to extremes.

Light

It is very important to monitor the light your indoor plants receive. Different indoor plants require different amounts of exposure to light. For example, a fern that enjoys shaded conditions will quickly burn if exposed to full sunlight. A geranium, which may enjoy a sunny kitchen windowsill, will grow long and lanky and will not flower if positioned in too much shade. So it is important to understand the appropriate light conditions when purchasing an indoor plant.

The majority of indoor plants enjoy a bright spot out of direct sunlight. Also, the majority of indoor plants should not be positioned in a part of a room which is too shady. Take into account that light levels are not as strong during winter months and that some of your indoor plants may need to be moved to brighter positions. At the height of summer, these positions may provide sunlight which is too strong and, as a result, plants may need to be moved again to avoid this.

Warmth

Indoor plants enjoy warm conditions. It is important to avoid draughts, which can cause chill. It's also important to keep your indoor plants away from a heat source, for example, radiators, open fires and even televisions or hi-fi's. Indoor plants are

Regal Pelargonium 'Springfield Black' which needs plenty of light to grow well

generally comfortable in the same temperature conditions that we enjoy ourselves. If a room is warm and pleasant to be in it is providing the right type of temperature conditions for your plants.

In winter, avoid placing indoor plants on a window ledge where the plants will be trapped between a curtain and window at night time. This area can become very cold and cause problems. It is also worth noting that indoor plants which are kept on the dry side will tolerate cooler conditions in winter than those which are wet.

Humidity

Our homes are designed to be dry and the forms of heating that we use to keep our homes warm create a dry atmosphere. This is completely alien to the majority of indoor plants we grow. These houseplants grow outside in naturally humid conditions somewhere in the world. So to deprive your indoor plants of humidity can cause severe problems. It is important to create some artificial humidity to assist them in growing healthily.

Here are a couple of methods which you will find useful for providing the necessary humidity.

● Double potting

This is simple and easy to do. By placing your indoor plant into a larger pot which has been filled with damp peat moss. This peat moss can be kept moist and as the moisture evaporates it helps to create a band of humidity around the plant.

● Misting

This is especially beneficial in spring when new growth is appearing. Lightly mist the foliage of indoor plants using water in a small hand mister. This can be done several times a week and is especially valuable on ferns and other foliage house plants.

● Grouping

By grouping your plants on a tray which is half-filled with gravel it is easy to pour water into this tray

Gloriosa superba 'Rothschildiana' – an excellent climbing plant for a conservatory. It benefits from occasional liquid tomato feed which encourages flowering

without submersing your plants in it. The water level should always be kept a little below the level of the gravel. This water evaporates creating the ideal conditions. In a warm room it will be necessary to keep this water reservoir topped up. The plants also benefit from being grouped together and will receive moisture which will evaporate from surrounding plants.

Feeding

Established indoor plants will require liquid feeding. This helps to sustain the plant, keeping it healthy and, if necessary, assisting in providing flowers. There are two main types of liquid feed for indoor plants – liquid feed which provides the necessary nutrients for healthy foliage and liquid feed which encourages flowers and berries.

When using liquid feed, it is important that the compost is evenly moist in advance, as liquid feed can damage roots if they are dry. It is essential to follow the exact instructions on the container as overfeeding can build up in the compost and kill an otherwise healthy plant. Feeding is best carried out when your indoor plants are in active growth. This is usually between April and September. Little and often is the best rule here.

Rest

During winter months, the majority of our house plants require a rest period. This is when they need less water, no feeding and most definitely should not be repotted during this stage. Usually by the end of March or early April you will notice signs of regrowth and then the process of increasing watering and feeding can resume.

Holiday Care

It just so happens that the majority of us are inclined to take our holidays when our houseplants are in full growth or flower and we worry about their care while we are away. If you are on a short trip or

Hippeastrum (Amaryllis) – Double red hybrid. This is a bulbous plant that benefits from an annual rest

certainly up to ten days and have a small group of indoor plants it is possible to stand them on a draining board, half filling your sink with water as a reservoir. Use a towel, placing it underneath the plants, with the other end dipped into the water. A capillary action will draw water from the sink through the towel and, providing the plants are firmly in contact with the towel, they will be able to soak up water as needed. This will keep them healthy until your return.

If you are planning a longer trip, it may be necessary to ask a neighbour, relative or friend to call and water your plants for you. It is a good idea to spend a little time with this person, explaining how you water each plant and each plant's individual requirements. Established plants can be quite valuable

Pelargonium sidoides – should be repotted annually to keep it looking at its best

and so it is worth going to a little extra trouble to guarantee their survival while you are on vacation.

Potting and Repotting

The ideal time for repotting an indoor plant is at the start of the growing season. April or May would be ideal. This allows the indoor plant to fully establish into its new container and compost before the end of the growing season. It is important to use a proprietary potting compost, using one recommended for indoor plants. If a plant requires extra drainage it may be necessary to add some grit for this purpose. The container can either be plastic or terracotta and ideally you should move up 1-2 in every time you repot. A good rule of thumb would be to pot a growing plant from a 3 inch pot up to a 5in pot. A 5in pot can be moved on in time to a 7in pot and a 7in pot can be moved to a 10in pot. Before potting on, the plant must be fully established, showing signs of its root system at the drainage holes in the base.

Pests and Diseases

There are many different pests that can attack an indoor plant.

Red Spider Mite

One of the most common pests on house plants is red spider mite. These are minute, tiny sap-sucking pests which usually affect the underside of leaves and the growing tip. The upper surface of the foliage usually becomes speckled with yellow blotches. Occasionally a very fine web may be seen on the upper parts of the plant. Red spider mite dislikes humidity and a deterrent is to daily mist your plant with water. A systemic insecticide will be required and may need to be repeated to eradicate this pest.

Whitefly

Whitefly can be extremely troublesome on fuchsias, begonias, busy lizzies and pelargoniums. The larvae live on the underside of the leaves sucking sap. Whitefly can appear in great numbers and spread from plant to plant. The adult is a tiny white flying insect. It is necessary to spray with an insecticide at three-day intervals, as it can be difficult to eradicate the larvae which reappear at this rate.

Mealy Bug

Mealy bug is a small pest which is covered in what looks like white cotton wool. They usually affect succulent plants or cacti and gather in clusters at the base or at stem junctions. A small infestation can be wiped away using cotton buds, but a larger infestation will require the use of a systemic insecticide.

Points to Remember

● Don't overwater

Remember that the roots need air as well as water. Keep compost too wet and you are certain of losing your houseplant. Learn how to water correctly and it is the key to success.

● Provide humidity

By increasing humidity you are giving your indoor plants one of their essential requirements. Don't forget that central heating dries the air.

● Repot when needed

Most indoor plants will require repotting every two or three years. Otherwise they can become sick and tired.

● Plants need a rest

This means less water and less feeding than when they aren't actively growing.

● Making the correct choice

Positioning a plant in the correct spot can make the difference between life and death, especially if the plant requires shade and you have positioned it in full sun.

● Look out for trouble

By being vigilant and catching signs of trouble early you can save a plant from death.

● Accepting loss

Some indoor plants are temporary and will only last a few months. These are generally referred to as pot plants. Consider them short-term and regard them as better value than freshly-cut flowers. Enjoy them while you have them.

Saintpaulia (African Violet)

Hints

Repotting

When repotting house plants, only do so into pots one size larger than the originals – and always take the opportunity to move the plants into clay rather than plastic pots.

Frost-free house plants

Move house plants into the room from windowsills at night in the winter – cold air from the window pane is trapped behind curtains and can cause damage.

Begonia rex – one of the most spectacular indoor foliage plants

Cactus

Don't disturb a Christmas or Easter cactus plant while it is in full bud as this is likely to cause the buds to drop. Succulent plants, especially species of cacti, should be given little or no water during the winter. Watering should begin gradually in the spring and a little liquid house plant fertiliser may then also be given.

Once-only poinsettia

Don't be tempted to try and induce a poinsettia to form its red bracts for a second year. It is very difficult to achieve without special equipment for careful regulation of day length. Keep it by all means, but as a normal, green foliage plant.

Wrap up warm

Always wrap a newly purchased house plant carefully in order to carry it home, especially in cold winter weather. Many potential Christmas presents deteriorate during a short, unprotected journey from garden centre to bus or car.

Pot-bound

If roots begin to appear through the drainage holes at the base of a plant pot, this is a sure indication that the plant is becoming pot-bound and should be repotted into a container one size larger, preferably in the spring.

Hippeastrum papilio 'Butterfly' (Amaryllis)

Pests & Diseases

Vine Weevil

Vine weevil has been the scourge of gardeners over the last twenty years. It has been responsible for hundreds of thousands of pounds worth of damage to valuable garden plants over those years. It is one of the most

Adult vine weevil and grub which cause unseen damage to root systems

common garden pests in Ireland. It is common in gardens throughout the country and causes damage to a wide range of plants. The larvae of the beetle will eat away at the plant's root system and suddenly plants like primulas collapse and come away in hand when tugged. The adult beetle is charcoal grey in colour and is nocturnal. The adults like to hide during the day, sheltering under leaves or in crevices in walls or fences. The larvae, which cause so much of the damage, are out of sight underground. They are cream-white in colour, have no legs and a small brown head. They form a 'C' shape and grow to approximately 10-12mm in length.

The vine weevil will lay up to 1,600 eggs over a three month period. The eggs are very small and are laid on the compost or soil surface, always very close to the stem of the plant, usually a choice plant and quite often one you have spent a lot of money on. The eggs hatch within 10-20 days and the larvae immediately start to work on feeding on the roots.

Damage is also caused by the adults. They can eat little semi-circular pieces out of the edges of leaves.

They are particularly fond of rhododendrons and the telltale damage is left to be seen long after the adult has disappeared.

To control this pest in containers, I have found Provado to be very successful. This is available from leading garden centres around the country. Follow the instructions and do not use on edible crops. Also from garden centres, you may be able to order a biological control called Nemasys. This should be used during warm weather conditions as it may not be fully effective if the soil is cold.

Slugs and Snails

Slugs and snails can be one of the most troublesome pests in gardens. It is never possible to totally eradicate them. No sooner have you killed one than there is another one to replace so the aim is to control rather than eradicate. The first rule when controlling slugs and snails is hygiene. Make sure to keep the garden tidy and avoid leaving leaves and decaying matter where they can hide. There are several methods to control this pest and I favour the organic methods.

- **Beer Trap**

  Fill a saucer with beer. Discreetly place this beside or under a valuable plant. At night the slugs will crawl in, have a party and drown. The next morning you can remove the drunken, bloated bodies. The boozy villains will all be dead. They will have drowned in an alcoholic haze.

- **Upturned Grapefruit Skins**

  These will attract the pests which crawl underneath for daytime shelter. You will need to collect the slugs daily and dispose of them for this method to work.

- **By Hand**

  If you are not squeamish, you can collect slugs and snails by hand. You will need to wait until dark and catch them by torchlight. They will be most prevalent on a dark, warm, wet evening when you will find them creeping up pots after your prized hostas.

- **Nematodes**

  More recently, a biological control for slugs has been developed. This is a natural and organic method and should be extremely useful on black slugs that attack potatoes. If you are a chemical-free gardener, this offers one of the best options for controlling this pest.

Slug

Chemical Control

If you are happy using chemicals, slug pellets offer you a further option. It is important that the pellets are kept away from children and pets. These need to be scattered sparingly. It is important to wear gloves and you will need to shake the pellets around the bases of vulnerable plants.

Greenfly

Aphids, commonly known as greenfly, are one of the most common pests attacking a wide range of garden plants and most commonly seen on roses. In warm weather they multiply rapidly and usually congregate on the soft new growth. If left unchecked, greenfly can cause distortion and stunting of growth. To control them, it is necessary to use a spray. Organic options are available. It is very important that these come in direct contact with the insect if they are to be effective. When spraying it is necessary to spray on the underside of foliage and to concentrate around new growth. Always follow instructions on dilution rates as a spray which is made at too high a concentration can cause scorching and burning of tender leaves. Never spray in direct sunlight. Avoid spraying on a windy day and always wear protective clothing and at all costs avoid inhaling any garden spray. Greenfly will need to be controlled on a regular basis. It may be necessary in summer to spray once a fortnight to keep them in check.

Hints

Damage on rhododendron foliage caused
by adult vine weevil

Checking for pests

When checking plants for the presence of
caterpillars and other pests, remember that they
are more likely to be beneath the leaves than on
top.

Red spider mite

Mist house and greenhouse plants frequently to
minimise the problem of red spider mites.

Woodlice

The best way to control woodlice is by finding
and clearing away their hiding places – under
logs, pots or piles of old seed trays, for instance.

Mealy bugs

You can fairly effectively control limited attacks
by mealy bugs on cacti and other plants by
touching each colony with a paint brush dipped
in methylated spirits.

Earwigs

Trap earwigs among dahlias, chrysanthemums
and other plants by filling plastic plant pots with
straw or hay and supporting them, upturned, on
the ends of bamboo canes. The earwigs will hide
in the pots during the daytime when they can be
removed and destroyed.

Caterpillars

If caterpillar attacks on brassicas become too
extensive to control by hand-picking, and if you
are not enthusiastic about using chemical sprays,
try the biological control method of spraying
with a culture of the bacterium Bacillus
thuringiensis. This is harmless to everything
except caterpillars and can be purchased from
garden centres.

Rabbits

To keep out rabbits, fencing must be buried at
least 1ft in the soil.

Dermot's Vinegar Spray for Fungal Disease

This is a great cupboard spray and I have
found that it works extremely well against
many fungal diseases. Mix two tablespoons of
cider vinegar in four pints of water and spray
the infected plant in early morning and early
evening. Try to avoid direct sunlight. This will
help to combat mildew and other fungal
problems which may occur.

Clematis 'Bee's Jubilee'

GLOSSARY

A

Annual – A plant completing its life cycle within twelve months from germination.

Axil – The angle formed by the junction of a leaf and stem, or lateral branch and stem, or of two veins where they meet.

B

Bedding-out – The placing of winter-tender and greenhouse plants out of doors for the warm summer months.

Berry – A fleshy fruit containing several seeds without a hard or stony layer surrounding them.

Biennial – A plant completing its life cycle within two years from germination; growing the first year vegetatively, flowering, fruiting and dying in the second.

Bulb – A modified underground shoot consisting of a small disc-like stem or plate, bearing several swollen fleshy leaf-bases or scale leaves, with or without an outer coat or tunic, and enclosing the next year's bud and flowering shoot.

Bulbil – A small bulb forming at the base of a leaf stalk, in the axil of a leaf or in the flower heads of some bulbs.

C

Calyx – The outer whorl of flower parts or the sepals.

Catkin – A tassel-like spike of small flowers, usually unisexual and without petals.

Chlorophyll – The green pigment of colouring matter found in the leaves and green parts of plants which absorbs light-energy from the sun to enable plants to build up carbohydrates.

Chlorosis – A plant condition in which leaves and green parts turn pale or yellowish, and may be caused by nutritional deficiencies, disease, virus infection, or injury.

Clone – A group of plants of precisely similar genetical make-up and identical, produced by non-sexual multiplication, usually by vegetative means, from a single individual plant.

Foxglove (Biennial)

Compound – Leaves composed of two or more leaflets; of inflorences with branching axis.

Corm – A short swollen underground stem or storage organ, of one year's duration, usually with a tunic, forming and arising on the top of the previous year's growth, close to it.

Corymb – A raceme or cluster of flowers with the flower stalks becoming shorter towards the top so that all the flowers open more or less at the same level, and are said to be corymbose.

Cotyledon – The first-formed leaf or leaves of a plant, present in and developing from the seed, usually differing in shape from true leaves.

Cultivar – Variety. A plant raised under domestication in a garden, or of a clone, or line breeding, or of uniform hybrid development.

D

Deciduous – Falling off; plants which lose their leaves in autumn.

Division – The splitting of the rootstock of perennial plants into separate parts, provided with crowns or buds and roots.

Drift – In gardening a term used to describe the possible carrying of chemical fertiliser, fungicidal,

Turk's Cap Lily (Bulb)

insecticidal or weed-killer dust or spray residues by air currents beyond the area of application; or of air-borne weed seeds from outside the garden.

Drill – A v- or u-shaped depression or shallow narrow trench made in the surface soil, in which seeds are sown, and then covered.

E

Evergreen – A plant retaining its green foliage for at least one full year or more.

F

Family – A group or related genera in classification; plant family names usually end in –*aceae*.

Fruit – The ripened ovary of a seed-plant, containing the seeds.

Fungus, fungi – A major group or phylum of flowerless plants, characterised by a lack of chlorophyll, and must therefore get their food-energy from other organisms, either as Saprophytes, feeding on dead and decaying organic matter; or as parasites, feeding on living organisms, including plants, and thus causing many plant diseases.

G

Gene – A basic physical unit of inheritance of living organisms, including plants, controlling one or more physical characters.

Genus, genera – A group of similar species with common structural characters found in the flowers, fruits and seeds.

Glaucous – Grey or bluish-green.

H

Habitat – The environment of a plant consisting of the climate, situation, soil, vegetation and natural factors to which it has adapted.

Hosta 'Halcyon' (Glaucous)

Half-hardy – Exotic plants which require protection during winter.

Hardening-off – A process of gradually accustoming plants to outdoor conditions of drier atmospheres, greater fluctuations of temperature, and exposure to more variable conditions after raising them under glass.

Hardy – Plants capable of surviving, thriving and completing their life cycle under the natural environmental conditions given them.

Heel – The small part of older tissue at the base of a young shoot removed from a parent stem as a cutting for propagation. Roots tend to form more readily from heeled cuttings.

Herbaceous – Annual, biennial or perennial plants which do not form a persistent woody stem. Of perennials plants which die down to the ground annually. Of plants which are soft, green and with the texture of leaves.

Herbicide – Chemical weed-killer, selective or total.

Hybrid – A plant resulting from the crossing of two compatible species or sub-species. Hybrids may also be raised from crosses between varieties of a species and different species of the same genus, or two species of different but related genera. A hybrid is indicated by the sign x. F_1 and F_2 hybrids are the first filial generation and the second filial generation from

Papaver (Herbaceous)

selected and controlled crossings of parent plants, repeated each generation.

I
Incurved – Bending gradually inwards.
Inflorescence – The whole flowering portion of a plant above the last stem leaves, consisting of the stems, branches, stalks, bracts and flowers.
Internode – The part of the stem between two adjacent nodes.

L
Laciniate – Deeply cut and divided into narrow segments.
Lanceolate – Lance-shaped, broad based, narrowing to the tip.
Leaf – A lateral member of a shoot of a plant consisting of base, stalk or petiole, and blade or lamina, though in many plants the stalk is absent.
Leaf-mould – The product of leaves heaped and allowed to decompose to an evenly fragmented mould or compost.
Loam – A somewhat elastic term for workable soils with a good mixture of the various sized mineral particles, ultra-fine clay, fine silt and sand, coarse sand and grit, plus humus-forming organic matter, ranging from heavy loam where clay is dominant to light loam with much sand. May also be applied to dark or black loams rich in organic matter.
Lobe – Part of a leaf, petal, calyx or other plant organ protruding from the rest of it by an indentation, divided but not separated.

M
Monocarpic – Of a plant flowering once during its life.
Monocotyledon – A plant of the smaller of the two Classes of Angiosperms, characterised by having one

cotyledon or seed-leaf in the seed embryo, by leaves which have parallel veins, by flower parts usually in three or multiples of three, and stem vascular tissue in form of scattered closed vascular bundles.

Arum italicum 'Pictum' (Leaf)

N
Node – A joint, or point on a stem where one or more leaves arise.

O
Organic matter, humus-forming – The dead remains of animals and plants in decomposition; vital to a fertile soil.
Ovule – The structure containing the 'egg' which develops into the seed after fertilisation.

P
Palmate – Of a leaf having five or more lobes from one point, hand-like.
Panicle – A branched raceme or corymb.
Perennial – Of plants living for more than two years, usually flowering each year.
Petal – A division or separate member of the corolla, usually colourful.
pH – A notation or scale used to indicate the acidity or alkalinity of soil. A pH value of 7.0 indicates strict neutrality. Higher values indicate increasing

Iris germanica (Petal)

alkalinity; lower values increasing acidity.

Pinnate – Of leaves having leaflets arranged along each side of a common stalk or rachis.

Pollen – Grains or microspores, containing the male gametes, released from the anthers of flowering plants when ripe.

Pricking out – The transplanting of seedlings from seed beds or containers to larger boxes, pans, pots or beds, to give them more soil space and living room. It is best done when first true leaves, after the seed leaves, begin to grow.

Procumbent – Lying or creeping on the surface.

R

Raceme – A simple, elongated, unbranched inflorescence with flowers borne on pedicels.

Radical – Of leaves arising from the base of stem, root or rhizome.

Recurved – Bent backwards with a curve.

Reflexed – Bent back or down abruptly.

Reticulate – Marked with a network, netted, often of veins.

Revolute – Rolled back and downwards.

Rhizome – An underground stem, thickening, rooting, sending up leafy shoots and flower stems from the end; lasting more than one year.

Rib – A main vein of leaves.

Root – That part of a vascular plant which develops from the radicle of a seed, normally extending downward into the soil or rooting medium to anchor the plant and to absorb water and nutrient salts for growth; the branching underground counter-part of the top growth, most actively growing at the periphery of fine rootlets equipped with root hairs.

Rootstock – A rhizome or underground stem from which aerial shoots arise. More loosely applied to the basal crown growth of flowering perennials. The stock on which a scion may be grafted.

Rosette – Of leaves radially disposed, usually at the base of plants.

Rugose – Wrinkled.

Runner – A slender prostrate branch, rooting at the top to form a new plant which can eventually be grown independently.

Wisteria sinensis (Raceme)

S

Seed – A reproductive unit of flowering plant, formed from a fertilised ovule; consisting of a resting embyo plant with a rudimentary root (radicle), rudimentary shoot (plumule), and one or more rudimentary leaves (cotyledons), enclosed in a protecting coat (testa), broken only by a minute pore (micropyle), and with a scar (hilum) where the seed was attached to the parent plant.

Sepal – One of the usually green, leaf-like segments which form the calyx or outermost whorl of the flower.

Serrate – Saw-toothed, with teeth pointing forward.

Sessile – Without a stalk.

Single – Of flowers with no more than the normal complement of petals.

Spadix – A fleshy spike-like inflorescence with flowers embedded in pits or sessile.

Spathe – A bract enclosing one or several flowers, thinly membranous as in Narcissus; leaf-like as in Arum.

Species – A group of

Lysichiton americanus (Spadix)

individuals which have the same regular and distinctive characters; the smallest group in classification.

Spit – In gardening, a spade's depth of soil.

Spore – The basic reproductive body of all plants but particularly fungi, ferns and mosses.

Spur – A tubular projection from a flower; also a short branchlet.

Stalk – A lengthened support stem of raised plant organs; a leaf stalk is a petiole; a flower-stalk a pedicel and the stalk to a cluster of flowers a peduncle; and a fruit-stalk a pedicel.

Stamen – The male organ of a flower, consisting of a stalk, the filament, bearing a pollen-producing anther.

Stem – The part of a plant which supports the leaves, and/or the flowers.

Stigma – The receptive part of the pistil on which pollen grains may alight and adhere to start the process of fertilisation.

Stipule – Outgrowths from the base of some leaf stalks.

Stolon – A creeping stem of limited life arising from near the base of a plant with a central rosette or erect stem; usually just above or on the surface, and rooting to form a new independent plant at the tip.

Style – The part or stalk of the pistil arising from the ovary of a flower to bear the stigma at its tip.

Subsoil – A non-scientific gardening term applied to the soil below the fertile top layer of soil.

T

Terminal – Borne at the end of a stem or shoot.

Tuber – A swollen underground part of a stem or root, with buds from which new plants or tubers are produced each year, and then dies.

U

Umbel – An inflorescence with flowers on stalks of similar length, arising from a single point, to form a flat-topped cluster; compound when peduncles also arise from the same point; and umbrella-like flowering structure.

Undulate – Wavy.

Begonia (Tuber)

V

Variety – Technically, a group of plants within a species or individuals which vary distinctively from the typical state or type of the species or sub-species. May also be used to describe a cultivar, a form or a member of a hybrid group. Abbreviated as var. or v.

W

Whorl – A ring of more than two organs or leaves arising at the same level.

Rosa 'Benjamin Britten' (Variety)